Minor Writings On Astrological Magic

Volume I

By Clifford Hartleigh Low

Edited by R. Weisserman

Copyright 2024 by Clifford Hartleigh Low

All rights reserved. No part of this publication may be reproduced, stored in a retrieval system, or transmitted, in any form or by any means, electronic, mechanical, photocopying, recording, or otherwise, without the prior written permission of the publisher.

Published in the United States by

Astrological Magic LLC,

830 E. Lawn Dr Teaneck,

NJ 07666 USA

E-mail: publishing@astrologicalmagic.com

Visit: www.astrologicalmagic.com

ISBN: 979-8-9893135-0-1

Table of Contents

Preface vii
A Note on Nomenclature and History viii
Why I Study Astrological Magic x
Why Medieval Astrology? xv
Resources Beyond Picatrix xxiii

Chapter One: How To Think Like A Magician 1
    What You Think You Know About Magic Is Wrong 1
    You Will Need To Study 7
    Nobody Understands Picatrix–With Good Reason 15
    A Brief History of Scholastic Image Magic 23
    Magic Has Rules 31
    The Consequences of Getting It Wrong 37
    You Are Not Alone 44

Chapter Two: How We Do Magic 50
    A Slightly Longer History of Scholastic Image Magic 50
    A Simplified Map of the Spiritual World 71
    What Are Celestial Spirits? 75

Chapter Three: The Nature of Talismans 90
    What Is a Talisman? 90
    Talismans vs. Petitions 94
    Elections Don't Make Talismans, But Forms Do 102

How Does a Talisman Work? 111

The Ideal Talisman...128

Chapter Four: The Construction of Talismans 144

How A Talisman is Made 144

Stones and Other Materials 154

Planetary Fragrances 160

Optimizing Your Talismanic Manufacture.......................168

Planetary Antipathies and Substitutions 175

Preface

This book began life online.

The posts are sourced from posts I wrote on two Facebook groups that I moderate, Astro Magic and Stellar Sorcery, as well as a web page I maintain at http://sorcerer.blog. It has been edited to make sense out of that context.

Although I have not used any of the text written by commenters on those pages, many of their comments and suggestions led me to consider the opinions and do much of the research herein. While they are too numerous to name individually here, I am grateful to their contributions and our discussions over the years that have led me here.

A Note on Nomenclature and History

The name of this tradition has mutated substantially since I was introduced to it around 2003. Chris Warnock originally called the magic of Agrippa, Ficino and *Picatrix* Planetary Magic or Renaissance Magic; restored to their proper historical context and with a bare minimum of anachronisms. I advised him that he was better off calling it Astrological Magic, as it was not being used by anyone else at the time (around 2006) and was far easier to find on Google.

Our agreement to use this term consistently has had many good and bad consequences, and almost nobody realizes that it is of relatively recent origin – though perhaps this publication will remedy that.

What had started as an attempt to brand Christopher Warnock's style of magic began to lose its distinctiveness in the public consciousness after a decade of expanded interest in this topic, so when I encountered the term Scholastic Image Magic in Frank Klaasen's book The *Transformations of Magic* in 2015 I attempted to once again rebrand the tradition. Unfortunately, this term had its own problems and I no longer use it in more recent writings. It does appear extensively in these books and has been retained for consistency.

The historically accurate term was the Science of Images. This term appears in many canonical texts of medieval and Renaissance talismans as well as the few texts of celestial petitions extant and pertains to both practices.

Which term will become standard is still unclear.

Why I Study Astrological Magic

In the early 1990s, I became increasingly active in the New York City pagan/magical community.

Our community had an adversarial relationship with law enforcement. Rule #1 was: Never call the cops, even if your life was in peril. They would almost always arrest you after planting drugs or on technicalities and multiply your problems.

Several serial criminals who preyed on pagans eventually became active in the area, learning that they could not be held accountable. Pedophiles, cult leaders, con artists, and people using magic shops as fronts for selling tainted heroin, crack and meth to young pagans were just a few of the most common types. Local activists- including myself- attempted to drive them out of the community.

After every attempt to drive them out ended in failure, I suggested to our network of activists since we had failed in using conventional means, we ought to try using our spellwork. *We were witches; why not use witchcraft?* Unfortunately, we had to admit pretty quickly that our magic either worked very poorly or not at all, especially against the criminals who had already become practiced in dark magic.

Leading this endeavor, I used my own habits and skills from lab experimentation as a former scientist to sift through the enormous amount of nonsense in print about magic and test it out on a daily basis. My aim was to find methods to objectively test the potency and reliability of the vast number of available magical systems, and then optimize their strength once worthy candidates had been identified.

But we lost that fight. We lost badly. By the end of the decade the community dwindled from about 10,000 people to around 500. These predators never faced justice. When they ran out of victims, they engaged in new scams or moved to other cities looking for fresh prey.

It seems as though because the practice of magic in the Western tradition has leaned so strongly into the Middle Class, relatively few people in it had to face life-or-death consequences of the failures of their magic. If enough of them had, perhaps we would have been better prepared.

While my efforts did not save the day, the realization that what passed as magic was offering false promises which could neither address small or large issues only motivated me to continue until I finally began making breakthroughs. Because I never gave up.

A particular turning point was my realization that I could save myself a lot of time and effort by looking at periods of history when magic seemed to either save communities in crisis or promote them dramatically to the apex of cultural dominance. Not personal case studies, but when a system of magic seemingly lifted the fortunes of hundreds of thousands suddenly- in ways that my older methods had failed to in New York City.

Two periods of interest to me were the Islamic Golden Age from around 700-1200 CE, and the Florentine Renaissance around the 1400s CE. An enormous amount of Astrological Magic material was produced before 1000 CE which was incorporated into the *Ghayat El Hakim,* and then around 1200 CE interest in this flavor of magic began to wane after being challenged by religious authorities. The decline of this style of magic and the end of the Islamic Golden Age piqued my interest greatly.

Of even greater interest was the centrality of Marsilio Ficino in the Florentine Renaissance; he not only was an open practitioner of Astrological Magic and advocate for his version of the same, but was an influential figure on numerous cultural and intellectual levels. If Astrological Magic could turn things around twice, perhaps it could do this again now?

After twenty years of obsessive research and the expenditures of hundreds of thousands of dollars in materials, I know that I've found what I've been looking for. But its perfect restoration has not been accomplished yet. That will take generations.

My interest and methods in evaluating magical techniques come from compassion towards people for whom magic remains a matter of life or death, rather than a hobby. It comes from a daily awareness that most of my closest magical colleagues are now dead. And I'd rather you who are reading this not join them too soon.

Can I do the thing I am attempting? Certainly not perfectly; but perfection is not required. This is only the beginning of a process which will enlist tens of thousands eventually. And because I know how serious this is, I absolutely *have* to try even if it displeases some.

In some quarters at this time the mere attempt to criticize and evaluate spiritual technologies provokes a negative reaction. That is because to many people systems of magic are very personal and analogous to religious faith rather than practical technologies. Ultimately the latter must prevail, because magic is a poor imitation of religion but potentially a far grander expression of worldly power.

I am here as a reformer of the practice of magic and its advancement, because it is so very necessary. If only we all had the luxury of believing that nothing is wrong! Cleaning out the stables of magic shouldn't be controversial, but we are now at a historic crossroads.

The reputation of Astrological Magic to be the supreme form of practical sorcery has grown over the past twenty years, but it has gradually disconnected from the catalyst which makes it work; which is to use the intellectual and astrological canon of the period consistently in order to replicate their results. There's nothing wrong with people mixing systems for their own esthetic or ideological pleasure, but claiming that they can also produce miracles thereby requires much skepticism and demands abundant evidence. After all, that has been tried many times before and consistently failed. Avoiding anachronism is actually our own sort of Philosopher's Stone. Without it, arbitrary combinations of astrology and magic can only produce mediocrity.

The reason why I study Astrological Magic is that upon extensive evaluation over twenty years it comes closer than anything else I've observed to provide miraculous effects with a high degree of reliability. It is not just another system. It is *real magic* in ways that very little else approaches.

It has the capacity to change the world in ways that we are barely capable of understanding yet. We are at the very beginning of a process of restoration which will take generations to complete and will be at least as impactful as the Industrial Revolution. It will institute a new Renaissance, the shape of which we now cannot imagine.

The re-introduction of powerful, reliable magic to world affairs promises to change everything.

Join me in this grand adventure.

Why Medieval Astrology?

I have very practical reasons for favoring medieval and Renaissance astrology in the construction of talismans and making celestial petitions.

Now, I don't mean that there's anything wrong with Hellenistic astrology, Vedic astrology, or even the countless permutations of modern astrology for natal readings. It's just not something I'm terribly into for my own purposes. I've had three natal readings in my life, and none of them really described my personality or personal history except in some very minor specifics. Natal astrology is undoubtedly real in the abstract, but I think the implementations all must have flaws, or I'd have gotten different results.

And that makes sense, because the evolution of natal astrology over the centuries is the result of people being dissatisfied and making changes. The oldest method is not always the best, nor is the newest; the best is the best, and I have not found it with any form of natal astrology. That might be a problem if I put a lot of focus on natal astrology, but I don't.

However, we are not discussing natal astrology, but the application of astrological elections and moments to spells and talismans which are useful regardless of someone's birth chart. So how do we determine which form of astrology is best for our magic?

While magic with some astrological considerations does appear in the Hellenistic era, we have not yet found any evidence of complex horoscopic astrology integrated into magic. The things called "talismans" during the Hellenistic period are either animated statues or the pendants the Persian Magi and their disciples wore to ward off "evil fates." The animated statues appear to have been hollow and filled with herbs and gemstones, but nothing contemporaneous suggests their assemblages were elected. The pendants worn and sold by the Magi averted evil fate, but that could be just about anything, including a prophecy of doom from an oracle; it may not have been anything astrological. It also could be; we just don't have enough information, ultimately.

Things changed dramatically with the rise of Islam. We have scant information about elected talismans before *Picatrix*; we have *De Imaginibus* of Ibn Hatim from about fifty years prior. *Picatrix* contains the *Agriculture*, and that must be older too. But our best evidence that *Picatrix* didn't arise from the void is that it's a compilation of 224 books which must have been widely distributed for a long time for the author to have had access to them. Some of those books, like *De Imaginbus* of Thabit Ibn Qurra and the *Agriculture* have been found separately, so the author probably wasn't inventing these texts. They're just lost.

If we take the author of *Picatrix* as honest (and I see no reason to believe otherwise), he was creating talismans and observing the effects of makers of talismans and celestial petitioners on a somewhat frequent basis. These practices were popular, and either openly done or as an open secret.

Most importantly, the effects of his magics and those of his peers are firsthand or secondhand, and very powerful-sounding. There was no doubt in his mind that the magic was real and was solving real-world problems in a palpable way.

Picatrix fell out of favor and was suppressed in the Islamic world, but it was transmitted to the court of Alfonso X El Sabio of Castile, and gained much prominence in its translation to Castillian and then Latin. Alfonso and his court believed it was a crucial resource about two hundred years after its writing, but it still didn't find the proper audience. Around the same time, Albertus Magnus experimented with talismans; their reputation flourished because of their presumed efficacy and the association with an extremely respected personage.

The audience was found when a copy of *Picatrix* fell into the hands of Ficino around 1480, or three years before he published the Three Books on Life. He adapted the talismanic recipes into medicines in his Third Book on Life, and the influence of this text was massive. Ficino's work as a whole kicked off the Renaissance, or at least fanned the flames- and that's when things got strange.

By the time of Agrippa's opus in the 1530s, he was talking about talismanic magic (and magic altogether) in different terms. In his books he would relatively rarely say he thought this recipe was validated by his experience, and instead would claim that his practices were things the ancients did or the Arabs were doing at the time. Some of this could have been caution about an accusation of heresy, but I simply think Agrippa believed that the glory days of magic were in the past and needed a restoration. He was convinced that magic was real, and had seen much evidence to suggest it, but a lot of the really powerful feats of magic used methods which as a Christian he could not perform, or simply involved lost knowledge.

This kind of hesitancy continued for centuries until the writings about Astrological Magic finally began to eliminate all anecdotes altogether and just provided recipes. After that came a silence of activity, at which point the Victorians like the Golden Dawn took over, using modern astrology which I have been convinced provides no useful results.

Throughout the medieval era, talismans and petitions were relatively commonplace. There are anecdotes to support that they were more popular in the Muslim world, and also more effective there. In the Christian world, talismans were seen as somewhat exotic and dangerous, but they had a foothold- all because of Albertus Magnus.

During the Renaissance Era, talismans as we know them were very popular in the Christian world, but writers also seemed to think they were not what they used to be. Some of this may have been the result of the clumsy de-Arabization of astrology during this period. The talismans in the Muslim world were heavily influenced by Sufism and Lettrism, and the elections were deprioritized as well as the materials. I strongly suspect that the results of this new wave of talismans were less effective, but there just isn't enough from that time and region translated into English yet.

That's why I favor medieval over Renaissance: All accounts suggest that the medieval magicians were making really kick-ass talismans and doing powerful petitions. The Renaissance magicians were making talismans which even they seemed to think were less impressive. However, they appear to have worked to some extent, or there would be a great deal more recorded skepticism. There's no evidence at all that the Hellenistic magicians were doing anything like this. Their magic was of other kinds.

My goal is to make powerful talismans and petitions, so it stands to reason that I would use the tools and methods of the people who made them the best. I think those were the medieval Astrological

Magicians, though the Renaissance magicians still have much to teach us.

Part of what I am attempting to do with the revival of Scholastic Image Magic is to reconstruct the methods used during specific periods and places which purportedly produced miracles on a routine basis. That alone is a very difficult task, because sources disagree, and translations are not always perfect. But when we mix periods and cosmologies, we can never be confident that our anachronisms are the reason why the spellwork failed or that the recipe itself is at fault.

Some people have a deep commitment to an idea, whether it's a house system or an overarching theory of reality. That's fine as a general life choice, but if we are attempting to be true to the intent of the authors of texts such as *Picatrix*, we should respect them by trying to immerse ourselves in their intellectual context.

To people who have been attempting to be thorough in our reconstruction efforts, when we see people adding outer planets or an emphasis on sect into the medieval and Renaissance systems, it's like watching a prehistoric movie where the Neanderthals ride pterodactyls and occasionally whip out a flip phone and call their robot friend. It's fascinating... but strange, and hard to justify logically.

I'm not saying people shouldn't or can't do it, but they ought to furnish some sort of rationale which can be explained to others of why they're mixing things up like that.

In my work and studies, I try to avoid anachronisms, and simply use *Picatrix* as a good foundation. While Hellenistic astrology is useful to me to understand how *Picatrix*-style astrology evolved, I'm not dependent upon it. The author of *Picatrix* and everyone else in the medieval era felt that the ancients got a lot of stuff wrong, and this was validated in the field in the context of creating and using talismans and petitions.

Now, I'm not a purist. I do find that several concepts in Hellenistic astrology and Renaissance Astrology and even Modern Astrology are useful, mostly in the context of things outside magic. I'm a believer in Renaissance Horary, I find Mundane of all types fascinating but intimidating, and people with certain Sun Signs put me off. And I admit to a certain fondness for memes about astrology. None of that is medieval.

But when I'm making talismans, I am a lot fussier and period-specific because my aim is to reverse-engineer what the magicians of the *Picatrix* era were doing to make them so powerful and legendary.

And it appears that I'm on the right track, because the talismans I've been making do things which are often hard to believe, but are quite real. If you don't believe me, give it a shot yourself and retain an open mind.

Resources Beyond Picatrix

It is admittedly difficult to begin working on Scholastic Image Magic without the right resources. Unfortunately, outside of Chris Warnock's courses, there is no real resource for beginners.

Even more important is orienting oneself towards the worldview of practitioners of the system. Thinking like someone in the 21st Century rather than someone in the 17th is a major stumbling block, because so many assumptions about the self, the universe, and metaphysics overall have changed that really do matter. There is much to un-learn before you learn.

Chris requires one of two books early on in his Astrological Magic Course, both of which are easily available. The first is *The Elizabethan World Picture* by E.M.W. Tillyard. It's a very useful book, but one of the most boring I've ever read.

The better option is *The Discarded Image* by C.S. Lewis. This book I can wholeheartedly recommend. It honestly convinced me that the pious Lewis almost certainly practiced some form of Christian Neoplatonic magic in secret.

I'd like to go a bit further and add two more books to your reading list, one of which is much easier to obtain than the other.

The first is the *Timaeus* of Plato and the many, many commentaries upon it. A great deal of the justification and rationale for (Traditional) astrology in Western Culture originates in this text, and it is profoundly elegant reading if sometimes a bit dry. You should read it fully at least once, but it certainly grows in value upon subsequent reads.

The second is *De Radiis Stellarum* of Al-Kindi in French, which has a version in English that is much harder to obtain. Though this text was certainly respected in the Muslim world, it was widely disseminated throughout the Christian medieval world as an explanation for magic which did not recourse to the evocation of demons and only mysterious natural forces. More relevantly, it's a logical philosophical and integrated view of how magic works, and is much more sophisticated than anything which has emerged since. Without understanding *De Radiis Stellarum*, it's actually very hard to understand *Picatrix*; and it happens to be one of the biggest skeleton keys to understanding the text for my own research.

Chapter One

How To Think Like A Magician

What You Think You Know About Magic Is Wrong

I usually start my astrological lectures with a version of "everything you know about astrology is wrong." That also applies to magic to some extent, especially magic which uses astrology as a key mechanism.

My friend John Michael Greer says that Eliphas Levi revolutionized magic by distilling it down to two principles; Will and Imagination, together bending the universe into submission.

The problem with this is that Eliphas Levi pulled this neat little definition almost completely out of his ass. Levi was much more of a theorist than a practitioner, and there's no proof (or even earnest claim) that he performed more than four spells/rituals/incantations in his entire life. That's not to bash him. He was a genius. But he invented what I call Victorian Magic, which is what most pagans or New Agers practice today. Its main tools are gestures, visualization, and sonorous gibberish. In spite of its relative newness, it does some really cool stuff and I use some of it every day. But it's not what the ancients called magic. It may be what the ancients added to magic to help it work a little better, like MSG in takeout Chinese food.

There's a passage in Agrippa which says, effectively, that magic is helped and hindered by the mindset of the magician. That downgrades the role of the magician's internal states enormously.

In Scholastic Image Magic, magic does not come from within.

Did you ever see that movie *Willow*? With the little person actor discovering (spoilers) that the finger which was most magical was his own? And it was a great revelation?

Well, Scholastic Image Magic is the total opposite of that. It's a great big fuck-you to the notion of magic promoted by DisneyCorp, as a metaphor for imagination and wishing. Because imagination and wishing can only get you so far. "If wishes were horses, beggars would ride."

Scholastic Image Magic operates on a very basic truism: Humans are pretty damn weak sauce. We are unique in the hierarchy of spirits in that we inhabit ambulatory matter, but that makes us a little more akin to freaks. Though there are some big footnotes and exceptions here, even the greatest of magicians is still basically just a weird monkey with a knack for deforestation. In the hierarchy of living things, we're somewhere in between God and e. coli- and probably a lot closer to the latter.

The universe is full of power. People are mostly full of seawater.

In order for us to overcome our incredibly limited nature, we need to obtain help from outside ourselves. Even moreso, help from beings higher on the cosmic ladder than us. Help from our peers won't allow us to go beyond our limitations in any meaningful way, because they share our weaknesses. Beings beneath us may occasionally come in handy, but there's a risk of getting dragged down. (Please immediately refer to Aesop's Fable about the scorpion and the frog, and apply this to all instances of demonic evocation.)

Nevertheless, using metaphysical semaphores (which is what I jokingly refer to the LVX gestures of the Golden Dawn) or the pentagram rituals, or the hexagram rituals, the intonation and vibration of YHVH or M.I.C.K.E.Y M.O.U.S.E. or whatever, is at best a bit of flourish and filigree in Scholastic Image Magic and astrological petitions.

You're welcome to do it, but if you're like me you'll recognize it's a waste of effort and discard it in favor of the many many other things you should be focusing on when creating talismans, making petitions, or even electing.

Scholastic Image Magic is much more physical than Victorian Magic. Words are important in petitions, inscriptions, statements of intent; but it's even theoretically possible to have entirely mute rituals, and have talismans created by some sort of machine and remove the human element almost entirely from the system.

(It probably impairs a talisman to create one silently or without any visualized intent, but it still would be a real talisman and it would definitely work. Considering that elections are often at 4am, I've definitely made quite a few talismans on autopilot that worked very well.)

The fact that astrological talismans by way of SIM are so material by emphasis is an advantage. Because it appears to be connected to the fact that when you need to use one, it doesn't care whether you're asleep or in a state of panic or unaware of the movements of the stock market; it's always looking out for you, calmly doing its job.

Getting you out of the equation is sometimes the best thing. You are not such hot shit.

After all, you're a weird monkey living on a speck of dirt in a very big universe. In order to get superpowers, you're going to have to do things which are very un-monkey-like.

A monkey can gesture wildly and hoot. Calculating time, using symbols, making tools, and asking for help from more advanced beings is beyond the scope of lesser lifeforms.

This is how you become a magician. This is how you get real superpowers.

(At least, in Scholastic Image Magic.)

Highly creative persons are no more magicians than they can levitate or raise the dead at will. Occasionally there will be overlap; a practitioner of magic will also be a highly creative professional in another unrelated realm. This is the exception rather than the rule.

Yet when you think about it, is it really a big asset for a self-proclaimed wizard to be talented at making shit up with ease? It might actually be a strong negative, like a "creative and whimsical" brain surgeon. It helps arm those who claim magic is deceit, or the product of an overactive imagination.

I blame Walt Disney, who helped popularize the notion that magic and the imagination were the same thing. There is too much conflation, and too much redefinition; and it is making clean research difficult. Magic is not a metaphor for something else. It is what it always has been; the mortal production of marvels by spiritual means.

One of the differences between ancient and modern magic is how you should govern your thoughts.

Modern magic relates in some capacity with the Law of Attraction, which finds its root in the works of Eliphas Levi. The idea behind this is simple: Will combined with imagination sets your course in life as well as in magic. If you want to improve your life or achieve a goal, you need to visualize or otherwise express positive outcomes exclusively. This has sophisticated manifestations such as Chaos Magick and unsophisticated manifestations such as The Secret.

Neoplatonic magic finds some of its philosophical basis in Stoicism. The Stoics advised the practice of Premeditatio Malorum. This is to say one should visualize all the possible catastrophes which might befall you, in the hopes that you will find them less fearsome when they occur – and also be pleasantly surprised when they do not.

This isn't a simple binary, of course. Certainly we are told in the canonical texts of astral magic that we are to keep our frame of mind in a state congruent with the spellwork we perform, and generally this means we should maintain a neutral or positive attitude when doing our magic. But the mindset of magical operations is not necessarily the mindset appropriate for the daily life of a magician.

True wizards begin their careers when everyone else's are winding down with retirement in sight. This is because magic is about wisdom as much as it is about power, and all the discernment in the world cannot compensate for the lack of experience of youth. Diane Duane and J.K. Rowling were both wrong about one important thing: There are no "child wizards", nor ever were.

If magic is not a metaphor, it is not the imagination, and it actually works, then the question still remains: What is magic? If not by imagination or metaphor, how are these wonders produced?

I think magic is the loophole in Fate, the escape hatch, the scaffolding behind reality, the machine code which built the programming languages which program reality. In a certain sense it's still predetermination, but at such a high order of abstraction that humans cannot understand it. It is effectively a counterbalance to Destiny, even if in some incomprehensible way it fits into the grand design.

You Will Need To Study

About twenty-five years ago I decided that it was time for me to investigate feng shui. That was the sort of thing I did throughout the 90s: I heard about some paranormal or fringe topic and I decided to investigate it, no matter how weird or silly. I'd balance skepticism with an open mind. It had proven productive on many occasions, and this habit is also what led me to astrology around the same time period.

I have to admit that I was wary; the entire concept of Feng Shui seemed painfully privileged. Only the very poor or the very rich seem to have a lot of living space and have no concerns about clutter. If you're poor, you don't have anything to fill your dwelling. If you're rich, you have a lot of extra space or can afford to throw things away and replace them when you're bored.

Still, the idea that a space has a flow of energy like chi flows through meridians in the body seemed plausible to me, and that it could be disrupted and mended also seemed reasonable. So, I was up for an experiment. I bought a used paperback on "Chinese Geomancy" for about a dollar, and studied it. I can't remember the author or the title, but it was for beginners. It was, if anything, a bit too simple for my requirements, but I didn't want to get overwhelmed either.

One of the doctrines of feng shui is that your home can be divided into nine zones, each of which signify some area of your life. If there is dirt or obstructions or things with the wrong color in a zone, it will bleed into the area of life it governs and cause problems. There are a wide variety of solutions, ranging from decluttering, redecorating, cleaning, and sometimes installing a curative object like a statue or a crystal. If you fix your space, you can fix your life. The nine zones are oriented to the entrance, so that the zone immediately to the left of the front door represents knowledge, and the middle rear represents fame and reputation. It's all the same for every home.

The problem was that the book wasn't quite sure where the entrance was supposed to be if you had an apartment that was in a larger building. Did you orient things based on your apartment's entrance, or that of the entire building? It seemed as though the author never fully considered that these would be in disagreement with one another; and my initial searches on the Internet provided no resolution to the conflict. (The Web was a lot smaller and harder to search through back then.)

As it happened, I was living in an apartment where the entrance was to the East but in a building whose front door was to the South. After ruminating on the issue for a while, I decided to use the apartment entrance to orient the ninefold subdivisions. One reason why I may have chosen the apartment door, other than it seemed logical, was that the area which governed love and romance was especially cluttered, dark and dirty – and that might explain why I was forlornly single.

After reading that book, I spent a whole day cleaning up that corner. I took everything out which could be placed elsewhere. I swept and then scrubbed the floor with rose water. I put down a floor lamp and screwed in a red party bulb. I took a vase and filled it with silk red roses and sprayed some perfume on it as well.

For science!

Now, the rest of the apartment looked like a war zone; but hey, at least that one corner looked and smelled gorgeous.

The very next day, I got a phone call from a woman DJ I slightly knew. She lived in the Midwest but found herself unexpectedly in NYC and needed to tell me something in person. Could she come over? Sure. It was a surprise but I was curious to see what was so urgent.

I'm not sure how that conversation began, but it very quickly turned amorous. Clothes were discarded. She had a lot of tattoos and piercings. I had the absolute best sex of my entire life with her.

She left afterwards, seemingly very pleased; and then she fell out of touch forever.

Needless to say, I was very very impressed with feng shui and wanted to implement the principles of it in every area of my life. I was thrilled. Was I the first person to figure this out? Feng shui was my new favorite thing!

But another shoe was to drop. Some time later, new articles on feng shui were posted on the Web which firmly resolved the whole entrance enigma. The correct way to determine the zone of love was definitely to use the entrance of the entire building; not the apartment entrance as I had used.

I had redecorated the area which influenced one's money, not love, and it was compatible with purple rather than red. It shouldn't have done anything. It's not as if decluttering and cleaning was bad, but it shouldn't have influenced my love life.

And yet, something definitely had happened. Within a mere day, a particularly hot acquaintance came to my home from out of town, screwed my brains out, and then went away happily. That couldn't have been a coincidence, and I'm still sure that it wasn't. The rapidity was highly impressive. But I was very confused for a bit.

The thing is, I was using the wrong part of my apartment... but I didn't know that. I believed I was summoning love into my life, and so it manifested. The symbols and correspondences had no inherent value-they had the value I had defined arbitrarily. And that's not feng shui at all. That's a different kind of magic, but magic it is.

Magic is not a unitary thing, and one of the big distinctions is where the power is drawn from. Most Victorian and post-Victorian magics draw their power from intentionality and visualization, and when you use that as a power source it has rules and limitations distinct from magics which tap into different fuels.

One of the patterns I observe is that Victorian magic influences the mind far better than material reality, seldom breaks natural laws, and even when fed power constantly tends to have a short life span.

That's why in retrospect I'm not surprised that my DJ friend developed a sudden compulsion to have sex with me and then exited the story forever. It was my visualization and expectation which fueled the magic, not the flow of energy through a space or any established correspondences. That latter set of circumstances might have produced a very different result.

When we operate using traditional Astrological Magic, we are not largely drawing our power from intentionality. We are drawing power from spirits of time and forces very much outside ourselves, and the limits of the self as a conduit don't apply to it nearly as much. This is why one of the traits of astrological talismans is durability; they cast influences for decades without interruption, and those influences themselves tend to be permanent or long-lasting.

You can engage in a mystical or magical practice and incorrectly interpret what is actually going on, even if you get a little of what you wanted. The result will inevitably be frustration, because it will be impossible to change the limitations of the chameleonic system. It is easy to get lost in the dark forest; stick to the well-trodden paths.

When you operate outside the established correspondences and rules, anything can happen. One of them is having a completely different system of metaphysics kick in and produce surprises- though usually it's a pretty bad surprise.

This is part of why it's useful to have a frame of reference in several different systems of magic, and a deeper understanding of how they operate. Because then a practitioner will have a chance at recognizing the traits of a system which is masquerading as another, using different sources of power, and operating by entirely different rules.

A lot of Astrological Magic out there today is something which looks like Scholastic Image Magic but doesn't work like it at all. And we should be on guard against this confusion.

Accept no substitutes.

Scholastic Image Magic is a demanding discipline to pursue. I personally think it takes about twelve years of concentrated study to master, and that's assuming the person in question has a great understanding of history and classics to start with.

The process of mastering electional astrology alone requires the employment of rote formulations hundreds and thousands of times until one begins to see hidden patterns, and correlations between stellar cause and terrestrial effect. You may or may not need a teacher or mentor, but chances are you do because the amount of material you need to internalize is both vast and superficially contradictory. (There are even potion recipes in *Picatrix* which are designed to fatally poison the smart-ass student.)

In addition to memorizing and internalizing astrological texts, it is required for the student to be deeply immersed in the culture and literary canon of antiquity, the medieval era and that of the Renaissance. And that's before you get to any of the magic. Magic during the era of the writing of the *Picatrix* was understood to be the highest of sciences, and incorporated all other knowledges within it. Which also means you're probably going to read countless passages that go right over your head until you've done your preparatory work, both in your understanding of other fields and your understanding of an archaic worldview. Not only do these authors make important references to texts and concepts that were ubiquitous then but not for centuries after, but the basic worldview of a SIM adept is quite alien to the modern mindset. Without comprehending these things, SIM will seem to be gibberish.

John Michael Greer describes the *Picatrix* and the SIM within as "medieval rocket science." Part of the appeal of this method of magic is that it is a great filter against lazy people, and people without intellectual heft. Not only is it extraordinarily powerful, but if you get to the point of mastery, it is a genuinely great personal achievement.

The author of *Picatrix* (and Agrippa too) made it difficult to understand many concepts, on top of all the other necessary learning. They did this to both create a filter against people whom they felt were unsuitable for the mastery of magic, but also to cultivate the sort of personality they felt was the ideal representative and heir to the mysteries within.

The obscurity was not designed to test the student's intuitive faculties. It was designed to test their intellectual faculties. You had to figure the damn thing out, like Sherlock Holmes not like Deepak Chopra.

I try to make this easier for you. That's because these and many other authors never really guessed that so many centuries later we'd have to not only master astrology and magic and ancient philosophy, but rebuild much of the canon and worldview which made it relevant.

I myself have far to go, though I have made great strides. Please try to recognize there is a path and begin walking down it. Wandering aimlessly based on whims and bad notions from fiction and games and other systems will never get you there; not even close.

Nobody Understands Picatrix-With Good Reason

Nobody understands *Picatrix*. Certainly not fully. It is one of the most cryptic books in history, similar to the Voynich Manuscript in terms of obscurity. People claiming to understand *Picatrix* are either trying to con you or are so ignorant that they do not understand how little they know.

I probably understand this book better than anyone else alive. I've read it thousands of times. But I only understand a portion of it. It's not because the book is badly written, far from it. *Picatrix* is very well organized. However, that organization is also partially why it's so obscure.

Consider the passage,"Why the secrets of this science may not be understood except a little at a time."

"The ancient sages who have spoken of the occult sciences and magic in their books wrote them as obscurely as they could, so that no one would be able to gain any benefit from them, except by means of wisdom and continual study and practice in them. This chapter is placed here, as though by mistake, in order to make a modest demonstration of this." -*Picatrix* III:4

Passages like this have led to the speculation that the chapters are deliberately arranged according to a cipher or algorithm, and the meaning of the text changes by the order of the chapters in the correct sequence.

While I have not deciphered this code, I have found evidence for it.

Some of that evidence can be found within particular chapters, one of which I lectured on. In chapter II:10 *Picatrix* goes on a discourse about intellectual fire, then describes the thirty-six decans and how to make talismans from them. These two topics seem to be unrelated, but are actually the same thing. It's just that the earlier section is almost totally incomprehensible without knowing that the intellectual fire is the role of the Sun in decanic elections, and knowing how it produces physical manifestations.

The seemingly random order of the passages and chapters are not sloppy work, but an attempt to hide secrets from the unworthy.

Also in that chapter, we have the infamous: "If there is one quality that is very abundant in its own remote place, its perfection is diminished and consumed in the way that health, after it is most strong, produces illness, and when fruits are ripe and ready to be harvested they fall off of the tree, and the little snake destroys and kills great snakes, and small and tiny worms when they join together kill a serpent, and the powerful is weakened by the weak according to his nature. You should carefully consider what we have said."

Nobody knows what that means, though I suspect it has something to do with how Terms work. *Picatrix* is full of strange and obscure passageso like this, and it's possible that even better translation will clarify things only a little.

The unreliability of some passages in our lapidary texts may cause consternation until you compare them with contemporaneous writings about animals, plants, and even the peoples of the world. Just as we read these latter texts with skepticism and discernment, we can use our noggins and sift fact from fancy in the lore of minerals.

There is fallacious information in ancient texts of natural philosophy as well as useful arcana. Many people in the ancient world were aware of these quirks, and copied texts faithfully even when they were dubious of passages in the belief that these references were symbolic or had some unknown value. Many simply felt they were harmless entertainment mixed in with useful lore.

One of the gemstones whose identity may have evolved over time is heliotrope, which today is generally believed to be bloodstone–but may not always have been fzal. What we do know is that when we make bloodstone into a Sun talisman, it does seem to provide the personal benefits described in Agrippa. But no gemstone I have ever heard of causes the appearance of an eclipse when it is immersed in water, or provides literal invisibility as the texts may promise.

Our lapidaries often describe gemstones as attracting iron as if they were lodestones, and yet without the appearance of such. Several stones are said to glow or burn the skin when touched;

perhaps these were radioactive minerals, but in most cases we have identified some of these as stones which are safe to handle. Many jewels are claimed to be found in the heads of animals, and this is unlikely for gemstones even if some mineral deposits do sometimes grow there.

Engaging in this tradition requires us to wrestle with complexity, and part of that is the recognition that our canonical texts cannot be held up to standards of modern perfection. That does not make them less useful, but only that they should be used as intended- clues to begin an investigation into the mysterious, not the final word on the topic.

A life of practicing magic and working within the magical community has taught me much.

I understand why the author of *Picatrix* was cryptic and evasive. He wanted the reader to *work* for the knowledge. It wasn't merely that the secrets were to be kept from the people who might abuse it; something you hear a lot in Kabbalah, incidentally. It was mostly something else. He felt that most people are undeserving, too immature, too caught up in their own pet theories about life in order to learn how things really are, how things really work. And what magic really is, and what it can do.

I've revealed to a very select few people some of the rather great successes I've had in the Art and Science of the Magi in my life... and basically, few of them believed me. They wanted hard proof, or they said it was mere coincidence, or it was going to happen anyway. Or they wanted to do it their own way; which between you and me will never, ever happen. And maybe that's justice. I aimed to achieve some of the more legendary feats of magic on a level hardly any people, even within the magical community, believe is literally possible. And I succeeded. And what did I get? Indifference. With little fragments of jealousy to spice up the stew.

I could not help but let a cold vein of bitterness entangle my soul somewhat. I'd originally thought the author was arrogant and cruel, but many experiences have led me to suspect that instead he was subject to the arrogance and cruelty of others. His reaction to it is manifest in the manner he revealed his knowledge.

I do understand why magicians sought to demonstrate marvels and wonders, because it is a simple human impulse to crave recognition for one's labors and achievements. But I also recognize that even though these demonstrations were achieved centuries ago, with greater ease, the numbers of true magicians were still very few. A tiny number had the character of a true magician, but most didn't even have the ambition and clarity to try or even believe.

It once seemed implausible to me that people would just fail to give a damn, or seek easy answers or have jaundiced motives, and that was why our predecessors were so peculiar in their disclosures. Now I understand, at least a little more. People have always treated magic the way they treat anything that is truly important; and it reflects badly on them.

The path of magic is not an easier one than others, and its greatest rewards themselves remain hidden. Magic protects itself.

A few years back I read some writings by Pat Zalewski, one of the most respected authors and preservers of the Golden Dawn tradition. He apparently doesn't believe in magic. He doesn't believe you can turn invisible, summon wealth, or any other thing. It's all a head trip; just a really good head trip.

It's entirely possible to have an illustrious career in magic and not actually believe in the reality of it. I don't just mean scholars, but hardcore practitioners like him. He's not alone. And many others believe in magic, but in a halfhearted way which is shallow because they've never had any dramatic paranormal experiences.

I am confident they are all nice people, but they don't have a lot to offer those of us looking for the miracle, questing for our grail. Their advice is going to be terrible when it comes to practical magic. If many of them encountered real magic like some of us have, they'd end up in a rubber room. And they really are the vast majority of practitioners.

When I say don't trust others, I mostly mean the mainstream of magic – in this narrow context. And of the rest, be selective. There are all kinds of people doing the real stuff out there, not all of them nice and not all of them particularly smart. And it's tough to tell which are which.

But don't trust yourself either.

Just because you're one of the fortunate few who have encountered or even mastered powerful magic doesn't mean you're immune to self-deceits of many kinds. In addition to the placebo effect, which we need to constantly guard against, I warn friends that "feelings are bullshit." What I mean is that without training your intuition, your intuition will not be a source of valid information. (And for the record, ancient Stoicism would have put psychic sensations in the same bin as emotions- things to refine and never be governed by.)

It requires minimal effort to design a ritual which feels powerful, but great effort to design a ritual which produces the desired outcome. Often an effective ritual won't feel like anything at all. It's nice when a ritual feels nifty and the results are powerful, but that's actually a rare combination. Appearances deceive, and that includes things our occult senses perceive.

Because belief is often thought to be a prerequisite of magic, and it certainly can augment it, it creates a situation where false attributions and confirmation bias can run amok. That's when magical thinking can turn into the more psychologically diagnosable kind of "magical thinking." And that's a bad place to go.

Just because magic is real doesn't mean that you can't get lost in your head and think that your own personal trip is magic. You have to be your own therapist on this one, most of the time. And just because you command gods and archangels in your ritual chamber doesn't mean you can be late on the rent or can skip taking a shower... Kevin.

What works for some is the use of the Magical Diary. Our memories play tricks on us, and if we write down events and effects we can use measurable dates and numbers to come up with something analgous to statistics to evaluate whether our experiences are normal or peculiar or virtually impossible. When you're doing money magic, using a financial ledger is also a great way to track whether your gains are typical or enhanced. When you externalize your experiences this way, that helps keep you honest with yourself and objective.

Another thing you can do is create a quarterly report card for yourself- to yourself. Create a system where you evaluate how you're doing in key areas of life; not exclusively the ones you're working on magically. You need to measure how you're doing, and if there's no average upwards trend it's time to kick the tires.

If your magic is powerful but you're stagnating, maybe you're missing something important. That's what happened to me in the 90s, where I was creating amazing spells which really did big things, which over time were totally inconsequential to my life arc. I couldn't understand why I was floundering if I had power. In 2003 I discovered Christopher Warnock's work and everything changed for the better.

If I'd been brave enough to write out an honest report card to myself and study it, it wouldn't have taken so long for me to make some changes. The challenge for most of us with this exercise is the courage to be honest to oneself and self-critical.

(And sincerest apologies to my former housemate Kevin, who I mentally used as an example while writing this bit. You did actually pay the rent on time, and your personal hygiene has vastly improved.)

A Brief History of Scholastic Image Magic

The tradition of Scholastic Image Magic began with its roots in Neoplatonism, and as such, it made some very significant changes as the world drifted in stages from polytheism to monotheism. It largely kept the Divine world in a separate category (in order to remain intact through various theological sea changes), but authors had a fair amount to say about it, even though it only occasionally impacted the creation of talismans.

Iamblichus is probably the Neoplatonist who had the most to say about the polytheistic divine world, where gods were near the apex of all the hierarchies. However, Iamblichus was of the philosophical school regarding the gods, believing that they existed in eternity and did not meddle in human affairs, but instead delegated daimons, heroes and so forth to descend into our world to influence matters.

The Neoplatonist and, broadly speaking, the classically philosophical take on the gods was that they were perfected beings, and as such most of the lore about them was allegorical rather than historical. They could not possibly have any negative traits, and anything which we as mortals perceived as negative was our failing rather than theirs.

Furthermore, the Hellenistic view was that gods which were equivalent in different cultures were very much the same exact beings, understood imperfectly. Zeus was Jupiter, was Amon, was Marduk. And yet none of these were planetary Jupiter. The ancient Hellenes would have felt the Babylonians were in error in their belief that the planet Jupiter passing the Descendant was Marduk entering our world or passing through the netherworld. But Divine Venus, the goddess Herself, was both unitary and multifaceted, in charge of planetary Venus.

A polytheistic model was most likely retained by the Harranian Sabians, but we don't know enough about their beliefs to be certain of them. They had temples to the seven planets and none to supercelestial gods as far as we know, so we have to assume that they followed some version of the Babylonian model where the planets were actually gods–though how they interpreted their passage under the horizon is anyone's guess.

The polytheistic aspects of astrology put the system in conflict with Christianity for many centuries, and a lot got modified or cut out in order to make it less controversial to religious authorities. That tension never really ended, but astrology did its best to adapt to changing times.

The main monotheistic view probably was codified by the Ikhwan Al-Safa and put into practice in the *Ghayat El-Hakim*. But there is clearly a tension between the polytheistic and monotheistic models here too, and the author of the latter often had to backpeddle and say that certain practices were "for informational purposes only" and quite haram for Muslims. But overall, the planetary rulers (not the planets themselves) were either angels of some sort or worked in tandem with angels. There's an odd tension in the petitionary texts when you don't know whether you're addressing the planet itself (and is that an angel?) or the angel assigned to carry out the works of that planet.

The Christianization of Neoplatonism was largely performed by Marsilio Ficino, and the question of polytheism was addressed in detail because Ficino was a Catholic priest, theologian, and proud Neoplatonist. He wanted to take the best of George Gemistos Plethon but avoid direct heresies. He may have been the originator of the idea that polytheistic gods of times past were actually angels and demons worshiped by ignorant pagans, the kindly gods being angels and the dangerous gods being devils. In his model, even the angels performing the works of the Malefics were angels, but he had to do some very slippery justifications for how the works of Saturn and Mars were a part of God's plan. His supercelestial archangels included some angels which did not fall clearly into any celestial category (which is why Michael is fiery and straddles Solar and Martial affinities) and others who clearly are the bosses of the planetary rulers, such as the Intelligence Graphiel being above the vicissitudes of time, yet directly governing the Martial planetary hierarchy.

In my opinion he gets some of this from Pseudo-Dionysius the Areopagite, though there is a debate whether the Intelligences of Agrippa correspond to those of Pseudo-Dionysius . I think they do correspond, because Agrippa cites him a lot, and they are described as so exalted and removed from the Sublunar that they can only be represented by number and ratio and never images, which connects them with both kameot and sigils. The grimoires which claim to summon the Planetary Intelligences in humanoid forms should be viewed very skeptically. They can't actually take forms. They're simply above that in the hierarchies.

Pseudo-Dionysius the Areopagite is an interesting figure because he was deemed authoritative by the Catholic Church due to his accidental misidentification with the original Dionysius the Areopagite. He said that the most exalted angels were the Intelligences, and were so close to God that in the past they were worshipped as gods–and while this was idolatry, it was somewhat pardonable because of the similarity. (This is some pretty incredible backdoor polytheism.) However, in his view, the Intelligences were outside of time and thus could not directly engage with our reality, and uniformly contemplated the One as their only activity. (In practice, however, I find they can engage with magicians even if it's a kind of passive reflex type of action or a delegated entity within time. I think they're pretty cool guys.)

Agrippa corresponded with Ficino, but it's tough to say if they agreed on everything. Much of the material on the planetary intelligences in Agrippa clearly come from some lost Jewish text which may or may not be classifiable as Kabbalah. Agrippa pairing planetary intelligences with planetary spirits–presumably demons or devils–overturns a lot of ideas in Christian theology, implying heavily that devils have an integral role in the running of the cosmos and are thus obedient to God.

Another problem in Agrippa is that he tried to wed Muslim Neoplatonist ideas about the planets with Jewish quasi-Neoplatonist ideas, and this was jamming a round peg into a square hole. The numerology of the kameot in Agrippa clashes with a more widespread number system for the planets (one of many, it seems) but this can be reconciled by saying that the numbers in the kameot are only of the supercelestial intelligences and not the planetary angels. But this is messy, and it just makes things far more complicated than it needs to be.

Another thing we see in Agrippa is the invention of angels for almost every possible thing, and it's not clear where most of them came from. I suspect a lot of them were just made up by Agrippa. This is clearly a reaction to Albertus Magnus being concerned that talismans with volition must be under the power of devils. By inscribing or invoking angelic names, talismans might be protected by forces hostile to devils-or at least make the creation of talismans less suspect. Nevertheless, this was imperfect protection against Albertus' concerns, because he would not have recognized any angels which do not appear in the Bible-or at worst the Apocrypha. Certainly, the angels which appear in *Picatrix* which have exclusive Muslim origins would have been presumed to be arch-devils.

Another thing I can add to this, is that when I am making Agrippa style planetary talismans with planetary sigils rather than full images I often add the sigil of the planetary Intelligence (but not Spirit/demon/daimon/devil.) I tentatively find that this adds a little bit of stabilization by drawing down power from the supercelestial realm, and overcoming minor electional flaws.

Now, it's pretty obvious that a lot of people have had personal interactions with divinities which correspond to the planets and they don't seem reconcilable with any of these guys. That's fine. There's a lot of space in the Neoplatonic context to keep your work with the celestial and your work with the Divine as integrated or as modular as you wish. Talismans and Neoplatonism can easily be seen as a set of tools, and not religious fact. Or they can be; this stuff is very easy to adapt for almost anyone coming from any perspective save perhaps pure atheism.

My own practice is pretty close to Ficino cosmologically, and I am a little distant from Iamblichus right now. I like the earlier Neoplatonists and wish they were more widely read. However, I have had enough encounters with polytheistic divinities to recognize that they're real; I just don't really get results from them the way I get from both supercelestial and celestial angels. Those act quickly and forcefully, and don't have incomprehensible agendas, even if technically they're more powerful.

We are used to seeing talismans with Hebrew and Latin characters, holy symbols and names, geometric shapes, and depictions of people, animals, and monsters all on the same object. But this was not the norm for much of history and is the result of the syncretic view espoused by Agrippa.

Albertus Magnus was concerned about talismans being hijacked by demons. His talismans were strictly ways of attracting or repelling natural forces; any spirit being drawn into a talisman would have to be a demon. In addition to forbidding incantations to appeal to non-canonical angels (which would have to be demons), and forbidding the inscribing of mysterious names on a talisman (which could invoke said demons), he also forbade suffumigations because these would be seen as a blasphemous parody of church incense (which would appeal to demons), and forbade the depiction of any living thing which was not from the natural world-such as a goat headed rider upon a dragon (probably a demon, or something attractive to them). The Albertine vein of this tradition would mostly be talismans with depictions of animals and people on it, and few words if any.

Another vein of this tradition appears to have been imported from some lost strain of Jewish magic. These are the planetary kamea, the Intelligence and Spirit sigils, and quite possibly the seals. The inclusion of Hebrew angel names and God Names are also a part of this influx. The reason why that is distinctive is that Judaism has strong prohibitions against depicting any living thing, especially during this time period. That is considered idolatry and punishable by death (if rarely enforced in the diaspora.) Jewish amulets and talismans as a result are almost always textual and geometric to escape the slimmest possibility of an accusation of idolatry.

By the time of Trithemius, magicians started combining the image magic of the Arabs with Jewish amulets and basically trying to forget Albertus Magnus' concerns. But it's important to remember that the talismans which involve kameot and text and the ones which were pictorial were seldom unified until the 1500s in the West. In the Middle East, where Islam was the dominant religion, these combinations were a lot more common because the restrictions of this religion differed greatly from those of Jewish and Christian magical practices.

Still, we see a sharp division between the magic of *Picatrix* and the magic of the Shams, the latter of which is heavily monotheistic and is a prime example of Lettrism–which some say is the Muslim equivalent of Kabbalah. The *Ghayat El-Hakim* did include religious elements which were excised from the Latin *Picatrix*, but both versions included a lot of pictorial image magic which seems to have less of a strong representation in the Shams.

Magic Has Rules

Magic has rules.

In addition to all the many hats I wear, I define myself first and foremost a *magical theorist*. I have spent most of my life investigating the hidden technologies and symmetries under the hood, to figure out how magic works in the first place and how we can make it better.

The idea that magic has no rules is a product of the realm of fiction. If you did something magical and it worked and can't say how, that's because you are in a state of ignorance not because "it's just magic." It's never "just" magic. We may not know the rules. We may never know all the rules. But in theory, they are comprehensible.

The only thing which has no rules is the Divine; whether you define that as a unitary God or a multiplicity of gods. The Divine can do any old thing it pleases. Magic is an expression of the Divine;

that is true. But so is everything else in the cosmos that we can observe. That doesn't mean there aren't rules to magic any more than there aren't rules to optics or gravity or any other lesser thing.

If magic has no rules and it is merely a heartfelt appeal to a higher power, then it is nothing more than mere prayer. If you believe that to be true, skip the incense. Skip the talismans. Skip the elections. Skip the nomina barbara. Just go to church. Or temple. Or the grove. Or the mosque. You'll get the same results, and save yourself a lot of money and effort. Which is best put towards faith anyway.

For me, faith is important. But I see that as distinct from magic, because I do expect the rules to matter and turn into palpable results. There's nothing wrong with having faith. But if you have faith in Divine justice, that's no reason not to use a lawyer, or go to the police. If you have faith in Divine healing, that's no reason not to go to your doctor. And so on.

Similarly, having faith in Divine miracles is no reason for you to avoid seeking relief in magic. Because waiting for Divine intercession for everything is seldom fruitful.

Magic has rules. Learn them and use them.

The matter of the Moon on the Ascendant is one of conflict between traditional sources, as I discovered while making one particular Lunar talisman early on in my magical career.

I favor *Picatrix*, which sternly warns against having the Moon on the Ascendant or even in the 1st House. The *Liber Hermetis* by contrast, seems indifferent to whether the conjunction of the Moon and fixed stars are on the Ascendant or Midheaven. It's possible that both are correct, and that the Moon is fine on the Ascendant for fixed stars and constellations, but I don't want to take the chance. *Picatrix* does not emphasize work with individual fixed stars but alludes to them only, so their quirks might differ. I think otherwise, but there is a potential loophole if one wants to risk it. In the interests of diplomacy if nothing else, I try to say that putting the Moon on the Midheaven is safer and better.

That's an instance where the Renaissance and medieval methods depart from one another. Chris focuses on the former, and I tend to use a mix of the rules from each period. That does mean the number of elections I find are fewer, and Chris' attitude that one cannot wait for a perfect election is understandable if one is pressed for time. I'm not always under such pressures, so I can put my attentions towards the most powerful talismans possible.

I won't deny that my Mansion talisman was strong, but it was strong in a manner which brought to mind the story of W.W.Jacobs' *The Monkey's Paw* (which every magician should read at some point, I contend.)

Now, there most definitely is a gray area between an imperfect benevolent talisman and a curse talisman. Nearly every birth chart could be considered an imperfect benevolent or malevolent talisman election; we are neither showered with gold when we step forward from our homes with every step, nor do safes routinely drop on our heads.

The rationale of talismanic elections is that the characteristics of the talisman's nativity fuses with that of the wearer. It only rarely has the strength to completely override the wearer's attributes, which are usually a jumble.

In many cases a talisman which has positive attributes but with afflictions will provide more good than bad to the wearer, and be worth it; a talisman with a weak Ascendant will tend to cause short term problems, even illness in the wearer, even if the Moon's state brings the objective to happy fruition. I wouldn't want to wear such a talisman indefinitely, but it might be acceptable to be used in an emergency.

My own strategy currently is to simply make every possible strong talisman and shelve it; either for an unanticipated need in the future, or for sale when I someday go commercial.

I don't think anyone following Chris's methods are fools. They are methods I myself used until only about a year or two ago, and I wasn't a fool then either. The sheer extent of *Picatrix's* electional rules are so overwhelming and intimidating, it's hard to incorporate all of them anyway- and I myself don't, partially because I don't understand all of them, and partially because the author is frequently quoting another text and may not have full confidence in it but merely aiming to be maximally inclusive.

What I do think is valuable is something I learned from that Mansion experience- a lot of magicians get so excited that their magic does *anything* that they cease to question why it is imperfectly satisfactory.

I do not buy into the notion that magic can only provide delicate pushes; that's a bit of a cop out and proof that technique needs improvement. It provides delicate pushes most of the time; but if that's all one achieves, why put in such effort?

To put it uncharitably, if your talismans for wealth are only providing a meager subsistence, if the people you aim to heal continue to sicken, and rites for love are not making dramatic improvements, *you are doing something wrong.* When people say that magic just doesn't do things more dramatically, or that sometimes Fate is unyielding, I am not impressed.

These things are technically true, but magic is not wimpy. Your own methods are. Fortunately, with determination, humbleness, and curiosity, all practitioners can improve and become powerful.

One of my axioms is that all magic is time magic. I don't merely mean astrology.

One of the quirks of magic is that you can perform a ritual in July to produce effects in August, a ritual that you began thinking about in June. After the magic works satisfactorily, you may find out in September that in order for the manifestation to have come together in that particular way, the ball had to have started rolling way back in January or earlier.

This is a troubling notion. It either means that you were predetermined to do the magic, which is a rational interpretation, or somehow the magic influenced *the past.*

Instead of imagining the flow of time in a unidirectional way, imagine dropping a pebble into the smooth surface of a pond. Waves flow outward from the impact in all directions, creating expanding circles. Our perception of time is linear and progressive, but even in traditional astrology we know that not every part of the cosmos behaves like that.

Above the Sublunar Sphere, there is no generation or corruption, and at the outermost layers of reality there is absolute Eternity- a concept which no human being can even begin to truly understand. We can only define it in opposition to what we experience down here. There is no past, present or future in Eternity.

The idea that our senses and perceptions are muted, even harmful, is a theme which runs throughout Traditional Astrology, going back even to Plato. So the idea that we might be completely blind and misguided to the nature of causality is basically a given.

Several years ago, when first experimenting with this Tradition I found something truly horrible in my birth chart- a strong indicator of a horrible death. A friend of mine suggested I do some strong magic to alleviate the effect. I was doubtful but scared, and gave it a whirl.

Several months later, I discovered that my calculations had been off and I didn't have the problem which upset me so. There was only one problem; I had performed those calculations in the exact same way previously and couldn't have made that mistake. And yet, now I got a wildly different result. My memory and past events were conflicting, and I hadn't dropped acid or had a stroke either. Or anything like that.

When I was younger I had experimented with magic intended to alter the past, which seemed to have results like this- but this was the first time I tried to use it to alter an astrological event. Perhaps I'm a little crazy, forgetful, or just plain mistaken...

But I think magic not only can alter the past, but does so constantly in ways we usually never notice. And furthermore, that it is reasonably consistent with the traditional outlook.

The Consequences of Getting It Wrong

During the 1990s, I identified a phenomenon which I called the Kinkos Magicians. A lot of people were practicing magic which had occasional signs of paranormal activity, but left nearly everyone stagnant and in many cases worse off than before. Since they were convinced that they were on to something, and there was a widespread belief that positive thinking was necessary for successful magic, they were in intense denial that they needed to make any course corrections. If they believed hard enough and long enough, invoked often and banished often, they'd be revealed to all as the masters of reality that they imagined themselves to be. For a time, they were my peers. We were deposed nobility, unrecognized for our omnipotence and sagacity. If only our advanced wizardry could pay the electric bill.

Unlike the rest of them, I was willing to question our assumptions and put aside a decade of hard work. Because I could see the big picture, and it was that magical power meant nothing if it could not improve outcomes. Results were the only thing that mattered, and certainly not personal affirmations, which is all what we were subsisting on. My new inspiration was the phrase "Do What Winners Do," which I borrowed from the world of finance. Not individual winners, because most famous magicians like Aleister Crowley were dishonest self-promoters. Instead, I looked at cultures whose magical advancements helped their people- and also cases where the degeneration of that magic had taken most of those benefits away.

That led me to speculate about two major historical periods: the very rapid spread and cultural advancement of Islam, and the Italian Renaissance. Both became especially powerful and influential around the same time as Scholastic Image Magic became either used by large numbers of people, or employed by the ruling elite.

I also observed something nearly as interesting: When this form of magic degenerated or fell out of favor, the expansion and advancement ceased, and in some cases even entirely collapsed.

Scholastic Image Magic seems to have coalesced around 800AD, with the rise of the Abbasid Caliphate and the founding of Baghdad, a notable center of learning as well as imperial government. The doctrines of the *Ghayat El Hakim* evolved over the next two centuries, and were likely finalized around 960AD. Around 1200AD the *Shams al Maarif* was written by Al-Buni, in part as a Sufi-inspired reaction to Scholastic Image Magic being insufficiently Islamic. Materials were considered secondary, Quranic verses given far greater emphasis, and the planetary mechanisms treated almost as an afterthought. The *Ghaya* and texts which inspired it were considered heretical, and Sufist fervor and Lettrist practices took over. In 1258AD, the Mongols sacked Baghdad and the Abbasids were on their way out. And I don't think that was a coincidence.

Around the same time as the *Shams* was written, the *Ghayat El Hakim* ended up being remixed by Alfonso X El Sabio's scriptorium as the *Picatrix*. Something was definitely in the air, because this was also the same time period that Albertus Magnus began to experiment with talismans resulting in his *De Mineralibus*. Something clearly went wrong, because if the *Speculum Astronomiae* is any indication he came to believe that talismans were real yet perilous, and Scholastic Image Magic gained an ambiguous reputation in Europe. *Picatrix* and the *Ghaya* didn't get a foothold. Ficino gained access to the *Picatrix* some time after the

Council of Florence in 1439, when he met Plethon. He wrote De Vita in 1489 and died in 1499, so this is a good representation of his beliefs near the end of his life. This book was very heavily influenced by *Picatrix*, and Ficino was almost certainly experimenting on patients as well as making staggeringly complex talismans over the latter part of his life.

Ficino could be argued to be one of the primary instigators of the Renaissance. The execution of practitioner Giordano Bruno in 1600AD may have been a factor contributing to its end. By the time Campanella was constructing his artificial sky for the Pope, he apparently didn't even consider using talismans. The window of the golden era of the (European) Science of Images seems to coincide with that of the Renaissance itself.

In any case, I'm not a proper historian. What I am is someone who had a pet theory that Scholastic Image Magic was one of several candidates for a system of magic whose proper adherence had caused the rise of empires and cultural evolutions – and whose abandonment led to a decline in fortunes. I felt (and feel) that something this strong, if applied with sufficient rigor, could also transform individual lives in as profound a way as it seemingly did nations, religions, and cultures.

All of that is as far a cry from the Kinkos Magicians as possible. This is why I'm doing this, and this is why I am such a stickler for details.

Magic which has invoked celestial forces has been going on for centuries, but for much of the past two or three hundred years it has been a consistent failure.

Growing up in the magical community, I was baffled why people were invoking Jupiter for money, Venus for love, and Mercury for wisdom due to the virtually 100% failure rate. From 1981 until about 2003 I had never encountered a person engaged in celestial magics who had had any plausible results from their ritual magic. At best, their claimed results were well within the statistical range of probabilities. Most memorable anecdotes actually were of conspicuous backfires and flops. They did have entertainment value, though. They kept doing these rituals because the prior several generations had done exactly the same, and we seldom questioned the credibility of their techniques.

Some of us participated in a revolution in practice around the turn of the last millennium, but I am seeing signs that many of us do not understand the importance of the restoration of traditionalism or why it was so newly effective. Or that there had been a dramatic change at all. I fear that the misapplication of terminology will lead to a new era of pseudo-Astrological Magic; a counterfeit which undoes the progress of the past three decades. Already so much of that history is being lost.

One of the main reasons why I'm extremely jaded and skeptical of the capabilities of the occult community at large is my own personal experience and life story.

My first spell was a demon summoning. It went badly, and the demon haunted my home with "special effects" very much in line with a horror movie. My passion for magic was inspired in part out of a need to banish this entity and save my family. Unable to do this on my own, I reached out to the magical community repeatedly over three decades. Nobody knew anything.

I consulted hundreds and enlisted the help of hundreds more. Still, nobody knew anything. Many believed they had power, but it was never tested in the field; they failed my test. The minuscule few who had power, just didn't have enough. They fled, baffled. And after three decades all of my friends had been driven away, all my close family and pets were dead. Dead. Dead. Dead. And I was next, because the occult community was absolutely useless.

What saved my life, or at least bought me time, was that I stopped trusting others and started solving problems for myself. I used my scientific training to sift truth from fiction in occult writings. Most other practitioners were using methods passed down for generations, without any field testing. I was all about field testing; my life was a constant field test. Even after that demon was gone, figuring things out in that particular way became an ingrained habit. And it has served me well. I hope it can serve you too.

I know I'm flinty at times. My magical maturation happened in a crucible. But I am tough about this because I care, not because I'm an egomaniac. The medicine you need is bitter, but I sincerely don't know any other. I wish I did.

You see, I believe that there are people out there who need money magic so they can afford a lung transplant–and soon. I know there are people out there who are on the run from real life murderers who need protection magic. I know there are people out there who are seeking fulfillment and are at the brink of ending it all.

They need powerful magic, just like I did. Demons, after all, come in many forms.

Those of you who accept marginal results, well, you're pampered. You have a luxury that you don't realize you have. You're more entitled than you believe. Please be courteous to those who have greater needs, or those who can satisfy them on occasion.

The magics I find most effective were developed by peoples who needed it to work or they'd die. Which kind of makes sense if you think about it. The magics developed in medieval Europe and the Middle East were in a time when life was cheap. Hoodoo arose during the horrors of slavery. Kabbalah was developed among people for whom pogroms and massacres were so routine, it was like bad weather. There was an unnatural selection of their magics. If the magicians survived, their methods were probably better than those who didn't. And those traditions were passed on.

I am certainly not the only solid magician out there. Not by a long shot. Most are the inheritors of these hardy traditions. When I talk about people in the magical community citing vague results and being unable to self-assess, I don't mean these people.

Magicians who are wonder-workers are still quite rare. I find them to be like me, meticulous, skeptical and tenacious. Ready for the next challenge.

Let's face it. We're in the middle of a dinky plague, but bigger problems are coming. Some of them are communal and some of them are individual. You're going to have to up your game to survive them. Chances are, your "results" probably aren't going to be enough. I'm just here trying to help you get ready.

You Are Not Alone

As an adult, my favorite museum is certainly the Metropolitan Museum of Art. But as a kid, my second home was the American Museum of Natural History. Going back there and revisiting all the old classics was truly a lot of fun. It's a sprawling place, and easy to forget the sheer artistry of the aquatic fauna sculptures, the scale of the dinosaur bones, the occasional very badly-preserved stuffed animal, and the section on climate, ecology, and agriculture. I get something different out of every visit.

The Hall of Gems piqued my interest during one particular visit because of my interest in medieval lapidaries and talismans. In particular, I fell in love with the giant yellow sulfur crystals and the shimmering aquamarine jewelry. Not that interesting magically, but aesthetically nourishing. It's a shame that they're going to completely remodel it; it had a wonderful retro-futuristic feel. In any case, we went to the mummy exhibition and it was a lot of fun.

In addition to a variety of human Egyptian mummies were a few sacrificial animal mummies. My mother was an unrepentant Egyptophile, so I was immersed in much of this since birth—and once even took a cruise down the Nile

Somewhat predictably, the exit of the exhibit led directly to a gift shop brimming over with Egyptian mementoes. Knowing that the Bast plushie, the scarab refrigerator magnet, or Anubis pendant could all be fun décor but equally repurposed into genuine magical objects justified a spending spree. My cradled arms were full when I approached the cash register and put down the subjects of my inflamed avarice.

The cashier did not initially catch my attention, partially because I were distracted with my booty, and because she was wearing work clothes and did not stand out. But I caught her attention, it seemed. She stared at the selection of purchases, and then her eyes shot to my hands on the counter, and then back and forth. Something was going on.

I always wear gemstone rings on all of my fingers (and swap them out every so often). They sometimes attract attention, but they almost never are recognized for what they are: exceptionally powerful talismans, homes, or bodies for celestial spirits, which assist me in many things.

"You shouldn't let people touch your rings," she said, sotto voce, with great sincerity and urgency. "They will lose their power if other people touch them."

She was right, of course. When I began wearing talismanic rings, I would refuse to shake people's hands, out of concern the rings would become inert and the spirits would leave. Chris Warnock urged me to never let anyone touch my talismanic pendants, but he never quite knew what to do about the unique problem of magical rings; I was left to figure all that out for myself.

This isn't an uncommon notion in ceremonial magic; the classic grimoires require that your blasting rod, black-handled knife, athanor, lamens, swords and so forth be made by your own hands from scratch, and that nobody ever touches them but yourself, or they will cease to function. Victorian era lodge ceremonialism retains a less-strict version of this too. Mojo bags and jack balls in Hoodoo have similar prohibitions. Astrological talismans are not terribly different, but they do pose social problems in a culture where refusing an extended hand causes an immediate affront. And often an irreparable first impression.

Eventually I began wearing gloves at all times—replacing one horrible problem with a slightly lesser one—and after years of experimentation finally discovered that there was in fact a way to protect talismans from the perils of foreign contact. (This turned out to be, somewhat arbitrarily, the rings of the 13th Mansion of the Moon. Arcane secret revealed!).

I was in a state of partial disbelief that the cashier not only recognized my rings as magical, but that she knew magical rings would be imperiled by the touch of others. It is not common knowledge, nor uncontroversial.

I quickly surmised that she had profiled me from my selection of items—it's even possible that she had scoped them out for herself at one point or other. They were virtually all replicas of magical tools which could easily be turned into the real things. Then again, ankhs and such aren't actually that weird in this day and age.

That still didn't explain her absolute confidence that my rings were special. The only way to explain that was that she was able to perceive that they were metaphysically active. She was very likely a practitioner, and a very capable one too.

Yet it was still somewhat possible that she was a New Ager who was fond of crystals, and was about to prescribe soaking them in salt water overnight to purge them of bad energy. Just because you can maybe sense something doesn't mean you know what it truly is.

I attempted to reassure her that I knew the danger of contact with "things like these" and had found a solution, but I don't think she quite processed that such a thing was possible. Her response was rather marvelous.

"I keep mine hidden." She tapped her chest and I could hear the jangle of jewelry. "That way, nobody can touch."

And then she leaned in.

"King Solomon," she said, with much gravity.

I gaped a little. I really needed to be sure.

"Do you mean like a pendant with King Solomon's image on it, or do you mean the Pentacles of King Solomon?" I said.

"The latter," she replied, with a conspiratorial grin.

"I have those too!" I said, and tapped my own chest and jangled right back at her.

We laughed together.

All right, then.

The Pentacles of Solomon are either astrological talismans themselves, or something very similar to them, depending on whom you ask and how they are made.

At that point the people behind us in line were getting restless and I didn't want to cause her to lose her job, so we quickly moved on. I really should have given her my card. She was capital C-Cool.

The whole incident was intense but dreamlike. I was giddy to find a fellow practitioner in a wholly unexpected place. I was also a little startled that I could be spotted so easily.

Normally, even at magic conventions, people don't know what the heck my rings are unless they are explained in detail. They also don't give off power that most practitioners can detect unless they're very familiar with the tradition and know what to look for.

Apparently, if you've worked in some varieties of Solomonic practice, you can develop that faculty. Which is a good thing to know.

We are everywhere. Hiding in plain sight.

Chapter Two

How We Do Magic

Originally, a Preface to a Translation of the Speculum Lapidum Vol.3 *Provisionally Entitled* The Borgia Grimoire.

A Slightly Longer History of Scholastic Image Magic

The third and final volume of Camillo Leonardi's *Speculum Lapidum* is a treatise of image magic—a series of essays on the theory and function of amulets and astrological talismans, and a lengthy compilation of recipes from many sources. Dedicated to one of history's greatest villains, Cesare Borgia, it has acquired a reputation for compiling the greater secrets of the black arts.

This treatise is far more than it appears at first glance. It is a key to answering many lingering questions about the creation and use of amulets and talismans. It offers new enigmas for any student of ancient magic, medieval and Renaissance studies, the history of science, and traditional astrology, to decipher. And it is an important historical document in the development of science and magic.

People have been engraving stones or casting metals to endow sympathetic properties since time immemorial. Most of these can be classified as amulets or charms. Their shapes were believed to produce influences, or the material from which they were comprised had inherent properties that today we would consider mystical. Sometimes materials and shapes were combined to produce what some believed to be stronger effects. Many of the recipes in the *Speculum Lapidum*, as well as other, similar volumes, are of this relatively simple formulation.

By 1000 CE, and probably before that in manuscripts since lost, this process of creating mystical objects was combined with the increasingly sophisticated branch of traditional astrology called "electional astrology"—the choosing of fortunate times to commence an event. As in a personal natal chart, unusual configurations of planets and signs could endow rare skills, characteristics, and luck. Timing the beginning of something, such as the founding of a city, the writing of a book, a marriage ceremony, or the signing of a contract so that the horoscope was helpful would lead to greater positive outcomes. Under complex horoscopic configurations, for rare and brief windows of time, magical objects could be crafted which were able to bestow highly desirable powers, some of which were of a marvelous nature or appeared to suspend natural law. These came to be called talismans—an adaptation of the Greek term "tetelesmenon".

The elected crafting of objects to imbue them with mystical properties became a significant component of one of the most influential and widespread systems of magic in history. It has been called the Science of Images, Renaissance Magic, Arabic Astral Magic, Stellar Sorcery, Astrological Magic, Scholastic Image Magic, and many other terms. Its influence spread until around 1600 CE, when it began to wane in influence, until almost disappearing in the nineteenth century. This art was practiced as far West as the early United States and as far East as medieval China. Yet until fairly recently, it has been all but forgotten.

Hellenistic cultures produced their own talismans in antiquity. Talismans of this era had protective functions, and had some qualities in common with living beings; they were said to move about independently, speak, sweat, or even bleed. Most of them were in the form of statues. Some Hellenistic talismans may have been created using special timing, but there is currently no indication of great emphasis or sophistication in this regard. In some ways, these ensouled objects foreshadowed what was to come later, and it is understandable why the term "talisman" eventually came to be applied more broadly to mystical objects of foreign origin. They all existed in a liminal juncture between inanimate objects and conscious life.

This same term was applied to objects sold by the Persian Magians (or by people claiming to be their students) from the time of Plato to at least the first century CE. These objects were said to avert misfortunes, particularly oracular prophecies of death or an astrologer's prediction of doom. Some astrological timing was used in the crafting of enchanted objects as far back as dynastic Egypt, but the association of magic and talismans may have been so meaningful that one potential translation for the term magâunô is "the adorned ones", the term which was Hellenized as "magos", Latinized as "magus", and eventually Anglicized as "magician". They may have been associated with the Zurvanite heresy, which revered a proto-divinity of Time as the father of Ahura Mazda and Ahriman. It is also reasonable to conjecture that people who principally worshipped a god of light and revered fire would give an inordinate amount of attention to the stars and planets. Nevertheless, while this is intriguing, it remains speculative. Over time, the term "magic" came to apply to an immense array of metaphysical practices whose origins had nothing to do with Persia, but it is telling that the "magi" of the Gospel of Matthew followed a star to Bethlehem to pay homage, which solidified the association between magic and astrology with the growth of Christianity.

As Arabic science grew in sophistication from 800 CE on, astrological talismans were engraved in gemstones, cast in metals, molded from wax or incense, engraved on mirrors, and occasionally carved in wood, but the basis of their power increasingly came from the rigor and precision of the astrological timing under which they were made. The Hellenistic science and Aristotelian cosmology of astrology provided a complex and rational basis for how talismans operated. Claims of origins or influences included India, the Egyptian Hermes Trismegistus, the Harranian Sabians, and were even falsely attributed to King Solomon, Plato and other philosophers. But the primary identification of astrological talismans with the Persian magicians remained for a very long time, as well as the linked notion that this was an ancient secret practice rather than a medieval invention.

Arabic science and philosophy provided new rationales for how spirit and matter could interact, using permutations of post-Hellenistic material science, mathematics, and the reckoning of time by the stars and planets. Metaphysics was demystified and became more akin to engineering. Astrology, which had previously been seen as an expression of the will of the gods, was now largely seen as a collection of natural forces, and could be subverted to provide different outcomes in the same way one could use herbs as medicines to extend life. The Hermetic arts came to be defined as the harmonious trinity of astrology, alchemy, and magic. Alchemy focused on the transcendental qualities of matter, and astrology focused on the essential nature of time and spirit. They found union in magic as an attempt to influence spirit through matter, and reciprocally to influence matter through spirit.

Many unified theories of metaphysics that coalesced during this era, such as those by Al Kindi in his *De Radiis Stellarum*, explained not only how Astrological Magic was a rarefied natural science, but that other forms of magic had rational and natural bases as well. It was in this period that highly influential texts such as the *De Imaginibus* of Thabit Ibn Qurra, the Treasure of Alexander, and the *Ghayat El Hakim* of Maslama Al Qurtubi were written—the latter, widely distributed as the Latin *Picatrix*, eventually became one of the most infamous books of "black" magic in history.

Picatrix was a miscellany of alchemy, Neoplatonic philosophy, spirit evocation, and folk magic. But it was its material on astrological talismans that was most influential, acquiring a reputation for endowing extraordinary power and mortal peril. In its theoretical sections, *Picatrix* described talismans and magic in a way very different from prior conceptions. Magic was the performance of wonders to turn the attention of mankind toward spiritual aspirations.

Talismans were "violators"—ensouled material objects given new forms during elected times that allowed them to absorb the characteristics of a powerful astrological configuration through the embedded spirits of celestial hierarchies. A talisman was very much like a living being: a spirit embedded in matter. By being generated at a chosen time, unlike life generated naturally, talismans have a much greater capacity for influencing people and anything else in their environment through a kind of contagion or refraction of astral rays. By combining the pictorial component, timing, material of the object, and additional factors with sufficient skill, a talisman could be made to do almost anything.

These texts began an early wave of transmission into the Christian West, in part through the famed scriptorium of Alfonso X El Sabio of Castile. Three volumes from the scriptorium—*Lapidary*, *Picatrix* and its follow-up omnibus *Astromagia*—had enormous influence in Europe. Venerated fathers of the Catholic church Albertus Magnus of Cologne (in his *De Mineralibus* and his *Speculum Astronomiae*) and his student St. Thomas Aquinas seemingly experimented with astrological talismans similar to those in *Picatrix* extensively before condemning the practice, citing particular texts or common accompanying practices such as incantations and suffumigations as particularly abominable and potential sources of infernal influence. Their attention strongly suggests the avid interest and wide distribution of these texts. More generally, the association of astrology with white and black magic stirred a cauldron of controversy for centuries to come.

Possibly in reaction to this condemnation, numerous compilations of shorter works on gemstones and images were prefaced with Al Kindi's *De Radiis Stellarum* as a manner of proactive defense against the accusation of magic being demonic, rather than being at the cutting edge of medieval science and medicine. This short text explained talismans in a somewhat more materialistic fashion than *Picatrix*, portraying them as repositories of concentrated natural power rather than housing potentially problematic spirit entities. Even more boldly, it claimed that the primary function of human rational consciousness itself was the practice of magic.

It was widely believed in the Christian world that many of the unfamiliar angels, jinn, and less categorizable entities invoked in Muslim texts were demons, and that any contact with beings of unclear nature was to be avoided at all costs. A great deal of scientific and astrological knowledge entered the West through the Muslim world, and was studied avidly but cautiously. *De Radiis Stellarum* logically justified natural magic, and put many at ease.

De Radiis Stellarum also envisioned a virtually animistic cosmos, where all material things emitted invisible rays of influence upon their environment. This provided a rational explanation for amulets, charms and other objects of power disseminating a real but subtler impact, without the higher order of complexity required for astrological talismans.

For a time, texts of Scholastic Image Magic, which was the Christianized form of Arab Neoplatonic astral magic, were seen as an alternative to grimoires that focused explicitly on more potentially perilous contact with spirit beings. Compilations of these recipes were particularly popular in the libraries of physicians, perhaps because of their avid interest in Arabic medicine and astrology, and for some conspicuous coverage of talismans for protection and as medicines. One of the common rationales for the use of talismans as a form of natural magic was an analogy with medicines; using nature against nature to prolong life and ease suffering.

Astrological talismans were popular, and their adoption increasingly public and brazen. In 1390 John Gower, a contemporary and friend of Geoffrey Chaucer, published the *Confessio Amantis*, an incredibly popular English guide to virtuous behavior. In Book 7 of the Confessio, the wizard Nectanebus teaches young prince Alexander of Macedonia how to construct fifteen talismans of the Behenian fixed stars using combinations of gemstones and herbs, presumably in the common form of gemstone rings with herbs beneath. The instructions said to have been given to Alexander are a variation of a very popular grimoire called the *Quindecim Stellis*. Medieval legends claimed that Alexander the Great's magical rings gave him the power to conquer the known world.

A significant turning point in the popularization and dissemination of the tradition of Astrological Magic and talismans was the meeting of the Byzantine Neoplatonist philosopher George Gemistus Pletho with Italian physician, astrologer, and scholar Marsilio Ficino at the Council of Florence around 1440 CE, where Ficino was persuaded by many of Pletho's arguments. Ficino translated Plato's writings from Greek into the more accessible Latin, but more controversially, he also translated texts by Porphyry, Plotinus, Iamblichus, and what would come to be known as the Corpus Hermeticum. Ficino's advocacy for Neoplatonism and the practice of magic within a Christian context eventually led him to write his masterpiece *De Vita Libri Tres*, which provided medical and astrological advice heavily integrated with his positive outlook on natural magic and talismans. If Ficino's goal was to legitimize and popularize magic, he was very successful.

The floodgates were opened. In the years to follow, the revival of Neoplatonic and Hermetic thought became widely influential throughout the Renaissance. Giovanni Pico della Mirandola and Johann Reuchlin added Christianized adaptations of Jewish Kabbalah into the stew of Renaissance magic, along with a slew of other contributors.

Johannes Trithemius of Sponheim and his work on angelic magic, sigils, and ciphers was especially influential through two of his more prominent students: Heinrich Cornelius Agrippa and Paracelsus. Agrippa's monumental defense of magic as a form of high philosophy fully reconcilable with Christianity, *De Occulta Philosophia* (published circa 1500 CE), coined the term occultism. It became a standard reference work on magic, and remains one of the best source books on Astrological Magic. Agrippa discussed magic whose powers derived from the natural world, the celestial realm, the supercelestial realm of the angels, and ways to blend them together in highly innovative forms. Paracelsus, or Theophrastus Bombastus von Hohenheim, was an astrologer, alchemist, and pioneering physician who used astrological talismans extensively to cure disease and promoted their usage extensively in his writings.

It was around this very same period that the *Speculum Lapidum* was written, yet medieval image magic texts also became less influential. Caterina Sforza, one of the most powerful adversaries of the House of Borgia, was an avid practitioner of alchemy and a user and likely maker of astrological talismans. Camillo Leonardi may have presumed this interest was shared by her distant cousin Costanzo II Sforza and initially wrote the book for him. When Pesaro was taken by Cesare Borgia, Leonardi dedicated the book to his new lord in the hopes that the topic would be of interest and win his favor. Borgia died shortly thereafter, so it is unclear if he ever made use of this book; however, it is inarguable that he was of a highly competitive, daring, and cunning disposition, and would surely have coveted anything which may have given his rivals any advantages over him.

One of the greatest intellectual figures of the Renaissance, the polymath Giordano Bruno, was both an Astrological Magician and partially responsible for its decline in popularity. Incredibly prolific and often deliberately cryptic, texts like his *De Umbris Idearum* blended the iconography of celestial images (talismans) with his implementation of the medieval Art of Memory. It was perhaps Bruno's brash attempts to unify Hellenistic, Jewish, Muslim, and Christian thought in the form of a new Neoplatonic synthesis of sacred magic that led to accusations of heresy and his trial and especially gruesome execution in 1600 CE. All of Bruno's works were put on the Vatican's Index of Prohibited Books. The Catholic church's harsh treatment of one of its greatest luminaries was a clear political message. Magic increasingly became seen as an ideological rival of Christianity, rather than an ally.

Astrological Magic did not disappear entirely, but it did increasingly go underground. Documented in *De Siderali Fato Vitandi* of 1629 and some additional sources, Dominican friar, astrologer, philosopher and theologian Tommaso Campanella was enlisted by the Pope in 1626 to perform a complex sequence of rituals to neutralize the influences of eclipses which he believed would be fatal to him. Rather than using talismans, a circular chamber mirroring the heavens was erected in which torches and candles were placed in imitation of the planets in a benevolent configuration where the Pope rested until the eclipses had passed. The Pope survived and was grateful, pardoning Campanella of various crimes.

Texts of Astrological Magic remained in circulation, but interest declined, along with interest in-and the standards of-astrological practices. In 1801, Francis Barrett published *The Magus or The Celestial Intelligencer* in English. Based largely upon Agrippa, it kept the basics of the system in popular consciousness in English-speaking countries. The founder of Mormonism, Joseph Smith, is believed to have died wearing one of his most prized possessions: an astrological talisman dedicated to Jupiter, derived directly from material in Barrett's *The Magus*. Where he obtained it is impossible to know today, but it is clear that the production and trade in astrological talismans was still practiced to some extent, if furtively. *The Magus* was not merely gathering dust on shelves.

One of Barrett's students, Frederick Hockley, assembled a massive library of occult lore that included a source work of Astrological Magic talismans (which some speculate he may have written), *Abraham the Jew on Magic Talismans*, though Hockley's focus appears to have been on mediumship and scrying. Much of Hockley's library became a key resource for the highly influential Hermetic Order of the Golden Dawn, and it has been credibly speculated that the cipher manuscript upon which the Order was based was written by Hockley as well. Only fragments of traditional Astrological Magic found their way into the Golden Dawn curriculum, however. The integration of astrological symbolism in Victorian lodge magic was highly idiosyncratic because the lineage of astrology had been broken or frayed, the rationales for the integration of astrology and magic were lost, and many canonical texts were scarce.

The gap between the practice of Astrological Magic as a living tradition and its revival was filled with myth and misinformation. A quick survey of the iconography of the magician in nineteenth century costumes for theatrical productions often shows a man wearing monk-like robes festooned with astrological emblems, slippers with upturned toes, an imaginative range of foreign-looking hats, one or more oversized gemstone rings, necklaces of medallions, and often a wand or rod-a jumbled welter of fading echoes from bygone times. The awareness that some people once truly practiced magic sputtered out. Wizards were as unlikely as unicorns and dragons.

While the practice of magic and occultism in some form began to make a comeback in the 1960s, it took decades for those seeking the wondrous magic of ancient legends to find their way to what practitioners of magic were really doing in the Middle Ages and Renaissance. For most of that time, students of the occult believed those secrets were lost for good. In fact, they were hidden in libraries, concealed by a language barrier erected by the steep decline of public education. By Eurocentric educational standards, studying Greek and Latin had become antiquated and relatively unimportant.

The revival of traditional forms of astrology began with Olivia Barclay's edition of William Lilly's *Christian Astrology* in 1984, and was amplified shortly thereafter by Robert Zoller's groundbreaking book *The Arabic Parts in Astrology: A Lost Key to Prediction* in 1989. This was followed by the founding of ARHAT, the Archive for the Retrieval of Historic Astrological Texts, in 1992, and in 1993 by the ambitious Project Hindsight, a plan to translate the corpus of Western astrological texts generally only available in Greek, Latin, and Arabic into English.

Zoller's work was a reaction to well over a century of diminishing use of predictive astrology, often prohibited for legal reasons, but also due to incremental compromises to the philosophy of materialism which had stripped modern astrology of its foundational principles. More importantly, Zoller began experimenting with Astrological Magic and talismans with his students in private, in part as an attempt to push back against the desacralization of a spiritual science.

One of these pupils was Christopher Warnock, who was the first to openly practice and teach an expanded form of Zoller's Astrological Magic in 1998, and to sell elected astrological talismans to the general public. His open advocacy for the revival of magic with a traditional astrological basis caused some controversy, but it also created a foundation for what was to come, providing the primary momentum for this revolutionary perspective for many years. In 2011, Warnock partnered with John Michael Greer to translate a clear rendition of the *Picatrix* in English, with the aim of making this seminal text vastly more accessible to scholars and practitioners alike.

The contemporary creation and practice of elected astrological talismans draws heavily from the work of Agrippa, with somewhat selective inclusion of methods from Ficino, *Picatrix*, Ibn Qurra, theurgical material from the Neoplatonists, and astrology taken primarily from William Lilly.

As the corpus of Astrological Magic becomes increasingly available in English, individual practitioners are emphasizing sources to varying degrees, especially when they appear to conflict. Some practitioners prefer the spirit model of talismans as described in *Picatrix*, while others prefer *De Radiis Stellarum's* energy model; most see these as equally valid. Some practitioners see the use of talismans as primarily a path to mystical states of enlightenment, and some primarily as tools for practical ends, yet most see no conflict and benefit from both.

The material basis for modern traditional talismans can be largely divided between those etched using a diamond-tipped stylus in precious metals, gemstones, or sometimes wax, and those cast from metal and wax. Paper and parchment talismans are also used, as are mirrors etched with acid. Different canonical texts vary on their emphasis regarding the relevant importance of the material a talisman is composed of. The *Speculum Lapidum* values composition very highly, sometimes even to the marginalization of electional timing—which would make many of these engraved gemstones charms or amulets, but definitely not astrological talismans by the conventional definition. Similarly, practitioners today have a diversity of viewpoints on what makes for a good astrological talismanan argument that has been going on for nearly a thousand years, and shows no sign of ending any time soon.

The celestial basis for talismans is more diverse, and some are more popular than others. The simplest in terms of electional astrology are probably those of the 28 Arabic Lunar Mansions or Manazil al Kumar and the 15 Behenian fixed stars; there are certainly more than enough recipes for almost every imaginable purpose.

However, the seven planetary talismans are more popular; they have a reputation for being versatile, fast-acting, and particularly strong, with a fairly extensive array of variant sigils and pictorial images to choose from for both ease and manifesting more specific effects. Planetary talismans are sometimes used to remediate problematic configurations in a user's natal chart.

The 36 Faces or Decans also make popular talismans. These are narrower in focus than planetary talismans, but sometimes more profound in effects. House-based talismans are extremely complex, and utilize the power of multiple planets in harmony to achieve specific objectives. Zodiacal talismans are less popular, but are primarily used as complementary medicines and have a wide range of complexity. Constellational talismans are also less common. Exotic talismans such as those keyed to a natal chart, geomancy, or a horary reading have their own advocates.

Last but not least, nearly every class of talisman can be turned into a curse talisman by alteration of the electional rules, and made to sow misfortune and destruction rather than attract power, health, and luck. This sort of practice is extremely dangerous and best avoided.

The common procedure for creating an astrological talisman begins with seeking an election: finding a viable window of time where planets, stars, aspects, house cusps, signs and many other features of a chart create a pronounced spike in power or fortunation which harmonizes with a celestial hierarchy, such as a planet or fixed star. Every type of talisman has a different recipe of requirements for its creation; most frequently the star or an essentially dignified planet must be on the Ascendant or Midheaven, with the Moon also fortunate. Some talismanic formulas only permit narrow windows of time, such as a five-minute window every few decades; others can be made a few times a year in somewhat longer time windows. This is a complex procedure and often requires years of study to master.

From these elections must be chosen one with the least severe afflictions, or impediments to manifestation. Without a viable electional window, everything else is irrelevant. The Astrological Magician may choose to create a talisman in anticipation of a need rather than seeking a particular solution, in order to accumulate a versatile set of talismanic devices to respond to many different potential needs. For some, the process of seeking elections is itself a mystic initiation. At the very least, it trains the mind to think in harmony with the celestial spheres and maximize the power of outcomes.

Further stages of planning involve the selection of sigils or pictorial images, names or words of power to engrave or cast, and the choosing of materials. Religious prohibitions may have a role in selecting the former. The goal is to have the horoscopic configuration be in harmony with the images and materials; if a talisman is a mix of celestial sympathies, it will operate poorly or not at all. Harmony, sympathy and organization are strength; disharmony, antipathy, and disorganization lead to inertia and ineffectiveness. A talisman whose timing or design is flawed will lead to undesirable outcomes, and may need to be buried or destroyed.

Some practitioners will often abstain from sexual activities, fast, or engage in celestial dieting in preparation for the creation of talismans. Celestial dieting involves eating foods or flavors associated with a planet, and types of meat and vegetables that are harmonious. Some will meditate and contemplate celestial images or music harmonious to the celestial hierarchy in question, while others consider this optional. Ritual garb is sometimes worn, though most frequently practitioners will dress in sympathetic colors and compatible symbols during the rite of talismanic creation.

Most practitioners will use petitional texts from *Picatrix* or the appropriate Orphic Hymn as an invocation at the very start of the electional window. Some will abbreviate these for time considerations or religious prohibitions. Most will also use suffumigations, or incense smoke in which the talisman is immersed multiple times during the creation ritual. This is believed to facilitate the transmission of spirit or astral light into the matter of the talisman and increase its efficacy. Once again, this is sometimes omitted for religious reasons.

The peak of power tends to be in the middle of the electional window, and this is usually the ideal time for the casting or engraving to take place. Engraving on a gemstone or precious metal is usually done with hairline incisions invisible to the naked eye; it is not for the human gaze but for spirits to see and enter the object, or to register a meaningful change in the nature of the material as a kind of artificial nativity. Some people prefer secrecy and subtlety in their talismans, whereas others prefer more vivid symbolism and may desire cast metal talismans that have greater aesthetic value as jewelry.

Pendant talismans are worn over or under clothing; most prefer under. Loose gemstone talismans can be carried, used in talismanic potions, used to project power over a room or an entire property, or be the centerpiece of a celestial altar space for devotional work. Many other types of talismans have their own forms of deployment. Talismanic rings are special in that they frequently benefit from having an herb associated with that celestial order placed between the gemstone or signet and the finger. This strengthens the manifestation and helps direct the power toward more specific effects. Some canonical texts require certain talismans be shown openly; others require secrecy. Some forbid any but the owner touching them; others function by touching others. Modern users of talismans vary widely regarding their uses and prohibitions. Some wear many talismans at once; others only a few. Some wear talismans following the appropriate planetary day. The cleansing and recharging of talismans, if done at all, is also highly individualistic.

Most, though not all, talismans operate by proximity. A talisman for wealth belongs on your person or in your wallet. A talisman to protect you when traveling belongs in your pocket or car, not in your living room. A talisman to guard your home against thieves probably shouldnt be worn as a pendant. There are exceptions to every rule, however; some talismanic recipes attract or repel, heal or harm at a distance. The limitations of this system of magic are few, but one is the distance from that which is being influenced. A practitioner may bind a personal concern or relic to a talisman to influence a person over a distance; this can work, but is less effective than closer proximity or contact.

The use of talismans of a particular celestial hierarchy frequently assist further magical work with that star or planet in a gradual growth of affinity, trust, and in essence a series of initiations into the deeper mysteries of each heavenly court. It is still a matter of debate how talismans interact with each other. How people use talismans is quite variable and extremely personal, and idiosyncratic procedures are understandable during the process of rebuilding a living tradition that has lain fallow for far too long.

A Simplified Map of the Spiritual World

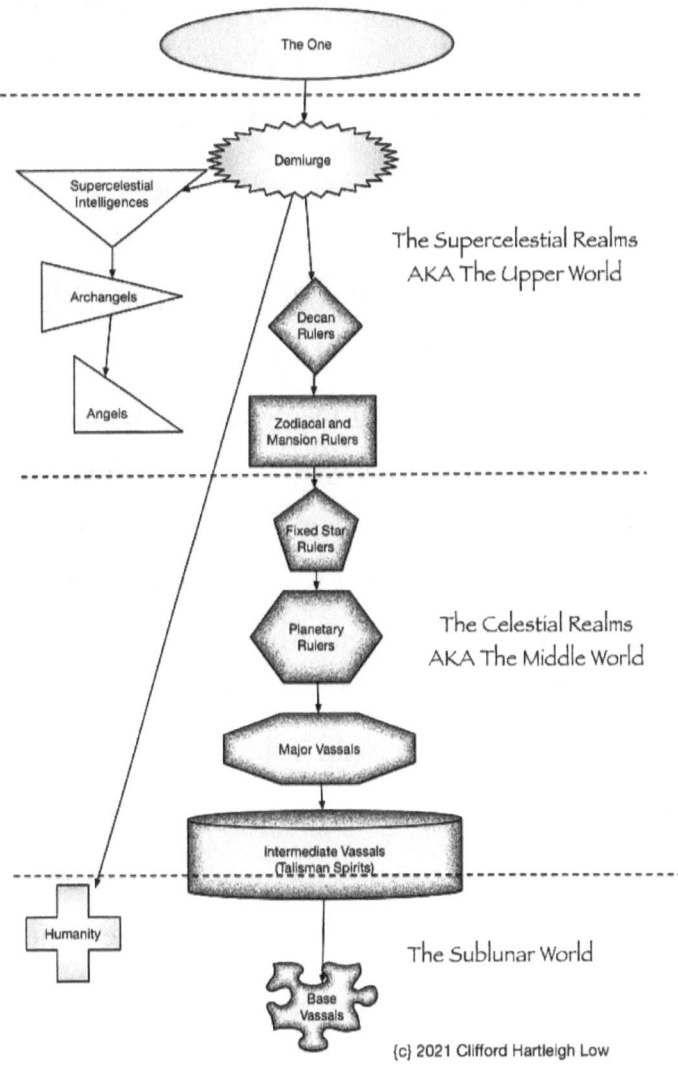

A disclaimer on this model, which I created largely for my own personal use and reference: It's fun to debate this, but the truth is nearly all of this is beyond human comprehension, and the models are never going to be fully reconcilable. My doodle above is not definitive because nothing like this can be, but it might be helpful to newcomers. This is a blend of what *Picatrix* implies and my own conclusions about Agrippa and Pseudo-Dionysius.

Some who are familiar with the use of the term "demiurge" through Gnostic cosmology may be familiar with the demiurge (specifically a being called Yaldabaoth in most interpretations) as a negative figure, but that was a minority view. The Demiurge is the primary creative force in the cosmos. While the One is supreme it cannot take action; the Demiurge forms all lesser things and is the source of the good. If you believe our universe is a prison, its maker and governor must be evil. But if you believe that the universe is neutral or inclined towards good, what set it in motion can be presumed to be benevolent. Humanity has a spark of the Divine, which is why there is a special relationship with the Demiurge.

We are never quite sure whether the celestial beings we work with are the same as the angels of religious and angelological literature. I think they are cousins, but not quite the same- yet not demons or jinn or the dead.

If Rulers and Major Vassals are human-like in consciousness, these are plant-like in awareness and probably are what power "talismanic materia." It's why they don't try to punish the user when they are consumed.

In order for anything to be affected by fate or magic it must have a spiritual counterpart. If a rock or a tree ever becomes relevant to any destiny or magic, it must have a spiritual presence. That means there must be a spiritual counterpart under any number of hierarchies present to endow it with traits and fate. This is also true in human beings, in the form of the planets within that make up the natal horoscope. But these energies or spirits are very rudimentary, and most have the intelligence of moss or bacteria, but they are governed by specific celestial forces. Celestial entities control nature, but their lowest servants carry out their commands. They are so base that they are immersed in matter along with us.

My understanding is that the Tropical Signs influence our reality only indirectly, through the interactions between them and celestial forces. They are forces of stability and stasis that are only expressed through interactions with visible forces of flux - stars and planets. That's why Decans need the presence of activating planets within them to potentially produce talismans. Without the stars and planets the Signs and Faces would be undetectable.

Now, one can percieve Signs and Faces with the imagination. Archangels and angels can also be perceived with the imagination, but the Intelligences cannot – and those are effectively polytheistic gods in a monotheistic framework.

It's a separate issue of where an entity is from and where it can go. So, for example the Celestial Rulers don't descend to the

Sublunar Realm but only send vassal entities (and usually the lowest ones.) On the other hand, Archangels and probably Angels are not subject to astral forces, and are thus beyond time and Supercelestial, but they can and do sometimes go slumming down into our Sublunar Realm on missions of various kinds.

One way I explain it to myself is that the Rulers of the 8th and below are delicate and would be disrupted by interaction with Sublunar matter if they could descend to us. They are composed of subtle matter (quintessence or astral light), which interacts with gross matter in many possible ways. The Archangels and Angels are not composed of matter of any kind but a higher order of light, and this allows them to (uncomfortably) descend into the Sublunar without injury.

The exception would be the Intelligences, which are so abstract that they cannot take any form and are basically living equations and cannot fully descend into the Sublunar, though they can influence events down here by mysterious means.

The quirk of the Intelligences is that in theory, they cannot take actions, but merely emit their influences in a constant manner- but in practice, they actually *do* seem to communicate and have self-awareness. That could be one of their subordinates acting on their behalf, however.

It's also not entirely clear whether the Decan Rulers are above the Archangels or not. The Supercelestial Intelligences are clearly above the Decan Rulers. The ambiguity with that is that humanity is superior to Intermediate Vassals but probably not Rulers. Yet Intermediate Vassals only penetrate into the Sublunar very tenuously in the form of talismans.

It's also interesting to note that while Rulers of one hierarchy can usually boss around Rulers of a lower hierarchy, it's not always the case for their vassals. A Lunar vassal can probably sometimes push back against a Mercury vassal, for instance.

What Are Celestial Spirits?

The *Ghayat* calls them Ruhaniyat, which is generally understood to mean "angel". But it's not that simple.

Picatrix says that talismans are possessed by spirits of time. What kind of spirits is unclear. Christian theology insists that angels cannot occupy a physical object. Albertus Magnus believed that if any spirit was in or attached to a talisman it could only be a devil, intent on deceiving the user. Instead it must operate wholly using celestial sympathies.

If you're not a strict Catholic, you don't need to worry about the acceptability of angels haunting objects, but it is actually possible for a devil to get inside or at least hijack a talisman. I've seen it happen.

Some years ago, I had a big problem that I could not solve alone and talked to a witchy colleague of mine who did a lot of demonic magic at ConVocation. She offered to put "a spirit" into one of my talismans to enhance its power, but was cagey about what sort of spirit when asked. Desperate, I allowed her to put that entity into one of my rings. I slipped the ring back on, and it deeply gouged the flesh of the finger. It began to bleed and continued to bleed for many hours. Nothing like that had ever happened before or since.

John Michael Greer was there; he did a geomantic reading for me. He said that the entity was malevolent and the situation was problematic. I went back to the demonic magician, and asked her to take her critter back. She smirked, removed it, and the finger stopped bleeding. She admitted under pressure that it was a demon after all, and she'd done this to prove to me that not all demons were bad. This was definitely not helpful to her cause, at least in my eyes.

Divination told me that the ring needed time to recover, and I put it on one of my altars for several weeks until it was ready to return to work.

What seems to have happened was that the devil and the talisman spirit fought for control of the ring, and my finger getting maimed was a symptom of their battle – or the discomfort and sense of betrayal of the celestial spirit manifesting through my flesh.

From this, we can guess that devils and talismanic spirits don't like each other, the way an angel might hate a demon and vice versa.

But it's way more complicated than that.

Both angels and talismanic spirits are personifications of natural forces. Devils in some traditions are fallen angels, but they do not fully control aspects of reality because their mandate to govern has been revoked. When they attempt to assume their former role or assert new privileges, they are fought by the divine. But the fact that they contest for supremacy over reality is partially why the Sublunar World is deemed Fallen. Thus devils have no legitimate authority over portions of reality, but constantly attempt to gain some manner of control over it.

If devils were assigned aspects of reality to govern, our universe would be a malevolent place, not merely Fallen.

The World in this particular cosmology (which has its base directly in Christianity, but potentially a different Christianity than any given reader may be used to) is a perfect Creation by God, and therefore the forces which legitimately govern it must also be benevolent. But there are attempts to usurp that authority, emanating from the False.

This is not to say that any being which accompanies unpleasant circumstances is a demon. Some aspects of reality are pretty awful, like death and warfare and disease, but they are necessary parts of existence. Angels of pestilence, for example, are not exactly good company, but they are a part of the greater good and grand design. Even angels of curse talismans can be understood to be doing "a dirty but necessary job."

And then we come across passages like this in *Picatrix*:

"There rises in the third face of Scorpio a horse and a rabbit. This is a face of evil works and flavors, and forcing sex upon unwilling women."

If the 3rd Face of Scorpio has a hierarchy of angels attached to it, the Divine has to not merely endorse this, but considers it a very necessary building block of reality. It's so important that an enormous tribe of angels are assigned to promote it, and presumably fight devils which attempt to thwart its fulfillment. That's when we get into some very dark territory, and the idea that these celestial entities are benevolent holy angels begins to tarnish rapidly.

Picatrix uses the Latin word for "ruler" to describe the monarchical entity which governs a stellar hierarchy. The Greek word would be "archon."

Those of you familiar with the beliefs associated with Gnosticism know that the archons are the bad guys. In the Gnostic view, our cosmos is a prison and the archons are the stooges of a malevolent Demiurge keeping us enslaved.

This naming is by no means coincidental. The surviving Gnostic scriptures describe the hierarchies of archons as celestial in nature, and corresponding to the governors of the Aristotelian cosmos. In their view, the Demiurge is not a personification of the Good, but an insane usurper, and his servants demons in angelic disguise.

What needs to be recalled is that the Gnostics were rebelling both against the Hellenistic Platonism of the day and more mainstream Judaism at once. Jehovah and the Demiurge were conflated, and then declared hostile, and the angelic hosts demonized as archons.

This view explains *Picatrix's* attitude that making petitions in a disrespectful way can get your mouth to seal up and cause you to die of fear, and if you make celestial petitions 99% of the time it will be denied. It requires very specialized timing and procedures to get a wish granted safely–which makes less sense if you're importuning highly benevolent entities.

Picatrix's attitude towards the spirits of time is a strange blend of Platonism and Gnosticism.

There is also a gulf between *Picatrix's* interpretation of *ruhaniyyat* and Ficino's reinterpretation of them as angels. Ficino's angels are holy and good, but the beings described in *Picatrix* are as diverse in manifestation as all of reality. And a lot of reality is very shitty.

Then we come to the Magians and their views, and that's when things worsen still. The Magians were Zoroastrians, and Zoroastrians believed that the entities which governed the planets were demonic not angelic. The idea that the planets are in aggregate evil turns up in other places, including the contrast between the constancy of the Zodiacal hierarchies and inconstancy of the planetary hierarchies.

The Jewish view is sort of an odd compromise. The most exalted angels are thought to be the holiest and most noble, but the least of the angels were almost indistinguishable from human beings- including a capacity for error. Do angels of the 3rd Face of Scorpio fit into the Jewish angelology better? It's very unclear.

It's also worth noticing the divergences on attitudes about the personal daimon among the Platonists before Iamblichus. Often the daimon's job was to force the human to endure their fates and were generally cruel, except to the rare enlightened man like Socrates. For many Platonists, the daimon is a devil.

We are still wrestling with the consequences of Michael Psellus, identifying the Hellenistic daimons of weal with the Jewish shedim of woe, as well as the blurry boundaries of angelhood.

So, where do I stand?

I think celestial entities are not Biblical angels, and not quite the criticism of them as archons either. They're not djinn. They're not demons. They're also not especially holy.

They have some common nature with Biblical angels, which are supercelestial; and they have a mutual enmity with devils.

They're... Something Else. They need a new category. Their job is to manage the material universe, which they do efficiently and mostly dispassionately. This perhaps suggests that supercelestial beings are doing some other tasks. It also suggests that the world we live in is not inherently good, but deeply flawed and not just Fallen. And these spirits are a part of the problem, even if they include many necessary evils.

They broadly dislike mankind. They find spiritus embedded in flesh to be an abomination, yet we can command them to some extent because we contain a Divine spark from supercelestial realms. This is why they are more frequently obedient to us in ways supercelestials do not; we outrank them, and we inspire a kind of jealousy even though they deem us unworthy. We can, in every version of the tradition, win them over by virtuous and prudent behavior. But it's not easy.

My practice is never to worship these entities, but request that they comply – respectfully and politely.

I also remind them, as necessary, that I have the authority to do so. Planetary spirits have a reputation of being moody and deadly. So, exercise caution.

"How to speak with Saturn. When you want to speak with Saturn and ask him for whatever you wish, you must wait until he enters into good condition... The most important point (of which you should take diligent care) is that you should see that the planet is in good condition and quality... because when he is like this, he is like a man of good will and a lively heart and a great and ample mind, and if another person seeks something from him, he cannot find it in himself to deny the petitioner. When the same planet is [afflicted] he is like a man full of anger and ill will, who is most ready to deny a petition." - *Picatrix* III:7

"Here, however, I wish to recount something that happened in our own time to one who wished to attract the virtue of the Moon, who performed this working for reasons of necessity, but spent a certain night living in a manner contradictory to this operation. On the night when he actually performed it, there appeared to him a man who had something in his hand, which he put in the mouth of the would-be magician; and at once his mouth was sealed up, so that he did not seem ever to have had a mouth. Thus he lingered for forty hours full of the greatest terror, at the end of which he perished utterly." - *Picatrix* IV:2

Most of the time during their course through the heavens, all planets are afflicted. Many sources consider peregrination as grave an affliction as detriment. Even if you exclude this and balance essential dignities with debilities, accidental debilities tend to cause more harm than accidental dignities cause good.

That's a good astrological rationale for why life tends to be shitty. If the planets are boned most of the time, our existence will naturally take their lead. This is a Fallen world, after all.

Picatrix in the earlier passage says that one should not ask anything of planets when they are afflicted. I take this to mean that any contact with the planet is to be avoided, but some think that it's safe or even beneficial to contact planets routinely.

The second passage is suggestive that this applies to contact, not just requests.

Attracting the virtue of a planet is not necessarily asking something of it, but utilizing it in some manner. This could indeed have been nothing more than an offering. But it was bungled so badly that a spirit slew the magician. While it's clear that the offense was not a bad election but incompatible behavior, it does suggest that extreme sensitivities do not exclusively apply to requests.

In any case, please do as you wish. I'm just explaining my rationale, and noting that in twenty years I've seen no compelling evidence to suggest that routine offerings to the planets do anything positive. I haven't seen anything particularly negative either, except that it became an expensive chore, and that will lead anyone to resent the planets whom the offerings are given to, a little bit.

One of the distinctions between magical objects in the Solomonic tradition and Scholastic Image Magic is the issue of "consecration", which in this context I am defining as a ritual which empowers or activates the object. The Solomonic method is fairly detailed and involved, but the Science of Images methods are superficially spartan or nonexistent. I want to explain why, because some find this confusing, or even an indication that SOI is underdeveloped–which is far from the case.

The angels invoked in the Solomonic tradition are beings which are very lofty and exist far above our reality, though some appear planetary on some level. They need to be forced or coerced into objects or to enchant them, because they normally exist in distant highly alien realms.

The celestial entities of Scholastic Image Magic are very different. They exist on a continuum of power, where the celestial Rulers cannot manifest directly in the Sublunar World but only send vassals to influence it; but the least of these vassals already exist on some level in our spacetime and matter. In fact, the reason why linear time exists and destiny and horoscopes are meaningful at all is because celestial entities and powers are interacting with us at every moment of every day of our lives. They are essentially down here already.

The process of creating a Scholastic Image Magic talisman is concentrating and optimizing that power, and embedding an entity which ideally is intermediate between those which forge our personalities and make the daffodils grow, and those which manage vast amounts of time and material reality like lesser gods. These intermediate vassal entities are far less alien than archangels who exist in the supercelestial realms. That's also why the material a talisman is made from is more relevant in Scholastic Image Magic- they are much closer in nature with matter than the supercelestial beings, and are correspondingly more sensitive to it.

Now, our celestial beings have a love/hate relationship with the Sublunar World. They find the generation and corruption to be disorienting and unpleasant, but they also find the sensations and embodiment overall to be highly stimulating. That is why consecration is secondary–they relish any opportunity to have a well-designed material body in the form of a talisman, and jump at the chance to go slumming amongst the Sublunar set. And they kind of like us, in the way we might like having a weird talking dog as a pet.

This is very different from the higher angels of the supercelestial realms, which find our world mostly repulsive and consider humanity to be glorified trash monsters who gained Divine authority through some kind of terrible cosmic bureaucratic accident. They need to be pressured to do their jobs, because they'd rather be anywhere else.

Celestial beings of Scholastic Image Magic don't need coercion, just good bodies. Coming down here is like a Caribbean cruise with less food poisoning. And we are the free entertainment.

When I was younger and working in different systems, I did get full physical manifestations as well as many instances of intermediate states between material and otherwise which had very strange properties. For example, visualizing the image of a talisman I was making, the details in my mind altered spontaneously and seemed to indicate the preferences of how the hierarchy wished to be depicted. It wasn't very different, just additional details that did not seem to come from me.

If you're doing rituals in an environment where there is a chance a person or animal might come across you (such as at crossroads), it's always best to talk to the being who approaches you as if it were a spirit. If it's just a person, you can explain why you addressed him or her like a crazy person later on. But if it's a spirit, addressing it inappropriately will cause irritation. It may even be a spirit partially or completely operating through the body of a person or animal, so it may have a very ordinary appearance. Even a police officer, which can get very nerve wracking. Spirits sometimes like testing the magician like that. It's also possible the spirit will spout nonsense. They're pretty strange.

When addressing stellar entities, aim to get the gender right. Many will withhold their full effects if one addresses them incorrectly. The gender of planetary entities follows that of the planet, unless the prescribed formula one is using is specifically contrary.

The gender of Face spirits appear to be all male, so far as I can discern so far. The gender of Mansion spirits default male, unless the formula is contrary. These react strongly to error.

The gender of fixed star spirits are all female. They are the handmaidens of the Sun. These react strongly to error. I have not worked with Zodiacal constellation spirits but I would assume they follow the gender of their associated Sign.

I once woke up from taking a little nap where I had a dream saturated with astrological symbolism where I was spoken to by a spirit of some kind. The spirit answered an important question of mine, or at least tried to. I posed the question to the ancestral shrine I use, but also at least on one other occasion to celestial beings. So, the safe bet is that this was a forgotten ancestor of mine, but could also be something malevolent or an angelic being taking a form I might find pleasant. The reason why the latter might be the case was the astrological imagery embedded in its appearance.

I'm close to ruling out that it was a natural dream; the entity asked me to repeat the answer to the question over and over, and this made me wake up. It's as if it knew that by doing that I'd be certain to retain the memory of the answer. That seems to imply autonomous intelligence, and alertness to the fact that I was dreaming but unaware of it- and skill in knowing how dreams and memory retention work together.

Based on its appearance, it was either an angel/daimon/demon of Scorpio or a dead magician with a close association with Scorpionic imagery. Lots of sharp, pointy things in his attire. It had the appearance of a human being. It was the clothing which was just slightly off from normal that made me think there might be something special about the person beyond what was apparent.

My intuition told me this was an actual benevolent communication. However, looking at the conditions around 10:20-30pm EDT in NYC, the Moon was combust right at the start of Scorpio, in the via combusta. Let's make it 10:20pm (near) NYC with 7 Cancer as the Asc on Monday the 15th. The separating conjunction of the Moon and Saturn was very notable. I have a reasonably accurate event timing, as Cancer was almost precisely on the Ascendant at the time I awakened. There was a pretty short window between when I awakened, got my bearings, loaded up SolarFire and noticed that the Cancer was on the Ascendant.

I do agree that divination is the best way to ascertain the truth ultimately, but I put more faith in my skill with tarot, runes, even pendulums more than horary at this point. I've just been working with them longer.

However, I do think it's important to research what stellar conditions are conducive to the manifestations of differing sorts. Spirits manifesting themselves to us in the Sublunar Sphere necessarily must be impacted by their passage through the Lunar Sphere and its state is one to observe most keenly.

Frankly, I didn't believe in astrology at all for most of my life until I went back through my notes and observed that nearly all spiritual activity of a dramatic nature happened when the Moon was in an astrologically distinctive state. Either the spirits wait for a propitious moment for whichever activity, or they can only act during hours they or their planets govern, or it's like a train arriving at a station; manifestation occurs when things just line up.

Chapter Three

The Nature of Talismans

What Is a Talisman?

A passage from page 27 of the *Picatrix*: "By sages, magical images are called talismans, which may be translated 'violators,' because whoever makes an image does so by violence, and makes it by conquering the substance of which it is made. To work victoriously he makes it with mathematical proportions and influences, and uses celestial writing. These images are made from their proper substances in order that they might receive the aforementioned influence, and this is done at appropriate times. By suffumigation they are strengthened, and spirits are drawn into these images.

"Know, then, that this is similar to the elixir, which conquers bodies and by transmutation changes them to other, purer bodies. Magical images similarly work in such a way that they accomplish all things through violence. Poisons work in a similar way, when they course through a body and change it, reducing it to its nature, because one body is changed into another by the power of the compositions that exist in it.

"You should know also that the power of purification that is called the elixir is made from earth, air, fire and water. These four powers become one in it, reduced to a common property and nature, because when it enters and penetrates a body it spreads through all its parts so that the body might better be altered and more readily obey and be transmuted under the elixir's power. Similarly, also, the elixir in alchemy works by quickly converting a body from one nature into another, nobler one, first overwhelming its harsh and hissing spirit, and removing its qualities and its dregs..."

The principles of magic illustrated in *Picatrix* are based on a model of order and disorder, hierarchy contrasting with chaos. Magic occurs when a ritual which is highly structured, every component corresponding with each other, all pointing in the direction of the goal-a goal which is the only missing link in the chain of being. The magnetism and eros which is the ultimate law of the cosmos forces that single broken link to mend.

The Sublunar world is understood as a zone of mixtures, and inertia, and chaos. However, the author of *Picatrix* looks at mixture as not merely conducive to weakness but is actually weakness itself. By imposing hierarchy and order into our reality, empowered by the true source of order and power–the heavens–it is the easiest thing of all to mold the world to one's liking.

What the author of *Picatrix* is saying here is veiled. He is not merely saying that one must conquer the matter of the talisman to endow it with power and purpose, but the talisman then becomes an instrument to extend that dominion outward into reality itself.

What he's trying to communicate is that the ritual and order doesn't merely transform the whole of the talisman into something new, but is how the talisman itself works on reality. It is a bit like a fractal pattern, operating on multiple scales. The institution of order makes the talisman changed, but its own embodiment of order is precisely how the talisman works to change the world in its proximity and do its work.

Talismans change entire zones of reality by making them rather like talismans themselves. A kind of contagion–like the author says– a poison, which suffuses within the body.

But the key to it all is an answer to a question that astrologers do not themselves think to ask. What is Rulership? What is control? Why are the cusps of the Mundane Houses so subject to the influences of the planets which Rule them? And why Rulership/Domicile, rather than Exaltation, which some consider to be stronger?

The answer is in this. There is a constant emanation of order filtering down from the heavens attempting to mold the primordial slime of the Sublunar world into kingdoms suitable to house the personalities and qualities of the stellar lords above. Rulership signifies control of an outside force, whereas exaltation signifies something else (embodiment of excellence, or supremacy.) Rulership is a story, a story of something enforcing control over something lesser on the Great Chain of Being.

Most people drift through life as if by accident, ignorant of power, perpetually weak, frequently controlled, and seldom even aware there is an alternative. Likewise, the nature of the Sublunar world resists this emanation of order, and this is the cause of a greater amount of the hopelessness, suffering, and meaninglessness of life. We live in a mausoleum.

Magicians have learned to institute stellar order, which is the mechanism of control, to abolish the anarchy of Sublunar life in a small way, to give meaning and purpose to the material cosmos. Because if magicians don't do this, the material cosmos actually has no purpose. It's void of meaning if left alone. So by controlling reality through instituting order, the magician benefits himself and infuses meaning and spirit through reality–not much different than pouring spirit into a doll of clay and bringing it to life.

We turn the mausoleum into a temple of life, a castle where the lights of heaven themselves descend and celebrate with us.

Talismans vs. Petitions

There is a great deal of misinformation out there about what makes something a talisman versus virtually any other type of object. When we use the word "talisman" as Astrological Magicians, we are not just talking about a fancy piece of jewelry. Nor are we talking about any particular magical object or artifact that may be created under specific astrological circumstances. When people think something called a "talisman" can perform miracles but don't understand the meaning precisely, greedy entrepreneurs can redefine "talisman" to be $2 worth of potpourri with a $200 markup and say it is a panacea. That is a degeneration. Accidental or deliberate abuse of terminology hurts people, because it makes everyone increasingly ignorant and all but a very few poorer and more frustrated.

Within the tradition of Scholastic Image Magic, a talisman is a piece of jewelry or statuary inhabited by a spirit of time which has a property of seduction, subjugation or contagion which overwrites reality in its proximity. It also has a quality of life because it can move and change shape and even injure the user if inclined.

"Know, then, that this is similar to the elixir, which conquers bodies and by transmutation changes them to other, purer bodies. Magical images similarly work in such a way that they accomplish all things through violence. Poisons work in a similar way, when they course through a body and change it, reducing it to its nature, because one body is changed into another by the power of the compositions that exist in it." -*Picatrix* I:2

The reference to poisons is a bit obscure, but important. The idea is that if you were to feed poison to a goat and eat of its flesh, you would also die because the flesh of the goat would not have been permeated with the poison, but actually *transformed wholly* into poison.

Elixirs transform things wholly into a new substance in an instant, in a similar way. Talismans work similar to elixirs. This explains some of why so many materials in medieval magical lore are poisonous; even in minute quantities, they are believed to harness primal powers of transformation.

Talismans will work automatically much of the time, but sometimes will do nothing at all without a request.

The Christian Neoplatonist view is that humanity has authority over the planetary hierarchies, because man was made in the image of God. Agrippa furthermore discloses that the Intelligences (the highest of angels, akin to gods, and associated with the kameot) cannot be commanded by mankind. The inference is that any beings lower than the Intelligences can or must be commanded by the magician.

The Islamic view of the *Picatrix* is more modest; talismans do appear to have some autonomous function, but large sections of the book are devoted to evocations of stellar beings and petitions to them for aid. These entities cannot be commanded, but can be beseeched for help with felicitous words, scents, costumes and materials; the inference being that according to the feudal model, the entities of the hierarchies can install the magician into their hierarchy as a lowly vassal.

What I can assert personally, is that on the occasions when I have used petitions they have proven highly effective, and on the occasions I have urged my talismans function for a specific goal this has worked – sometimes within mere hours.

Unfortunately, the term "petition" seems to be having a degeneration as well. Within the Scholastic Image Magic tradition, there are only two uses of "petition" which are canonical. The first are elected ritual conjurations where the magician evokes a celestial entity during an election and requests a wish be granted. Sometimes the entity is visible and sometimes it isn't. A large portion of *Picatrix* is devoted to these procedures; probably more than talismans.

The second are engravings made on talismans which command it to perform a specific function, often upon a person. (This is rarely done because there's so little surface area on most talismans.)

You can definitely ask your talisman to do something for you, but that's not a petition. It's a command or a request–or if it's weird, it's an incantation.

So why is this difference important, anyway?

It's all about power levels.

I can do a Saturn petition of the first type to cause a global pandemic, though of course that would be morally dubious. I can do a Jupiter petition of the first type to speed the process of finding a cure for that pandemic. If the procedure is good, either will come to pass. (I have done many things on that scale before, very successfully–however, I have not actually been the one to cause any global pandemics.)

I can make a Saturn talisman and engrave on it the petition "Cause a pandemic." It will not work. I can make a Jupiter talisman and engrave on it the petition "Cure the pandemic" and it will not work. However, if I were to engrave on either "Protect me from this pandemic," it probably would work–if it's well-made in a general sense.

If you take your Saturn or Jupiter talisman and hold it up and ask it, "Protect me from this pandemic" it probably won't work. On the other hand, if you take either talisman and hold it up and ask it "protect me from the pandemic at an important gathering next month," it just might.

We definitely use *words* iin most aspects of this tradition. But they are not petitions, and calling them that will cause a lot of confusion and ultimately disappointment.

If you think holding your Jupiter talisman up and "petitioning" it for a million bucks will do anything, you will be disappointed. If you don't understand that this is not how it works, you may conclude the whole of Astrological Magic is fake and find a new hobby. I see a lot of that happening.

If you do a formal petition with all the bells and whistles to summon a celestial spirit, you may become fabulously rich or richer. That's the kind of thing I do all the time for clients.

I've probably done a lot more work implementing the celestial petitions in *Picatrix* than anyone else, primarily in III:7. I do find it interesting that it collects much more than seven petitions for the planets, only one petition for a fixed star (which has proven difficult to identify and implement), and no petitions for constellations, decans, or any other celestial phenomenon. In other chapters we do see examples of petitions for the Moon as she passes through each of the twelve Signs. These petitions are not only very hard to implement due to the animal sacrifices required, but there is little guidance on what each of them are to be used for.

We also see rituals analogous to petitions, or at least with a very different structure, which invite the planetary spirits to appear visibly in III:9 and share a meal with the petitioner. As far as I know nobody has gotten the spirits to appear or have their petition granted so far, but that may change someday once the puzzle is cracked.

Chris Warnock has said several times in public and in private that he makes offerings to the 3rd Lunar Mansion spirit and gains financial benefits during her time once every Lunar month. I see no reason to doubt this, but it's not quite the same thing as a petition where one asks for specific boons whose granting can be measured. Chris doesn't generally ask for things, but is content to receive what the spirits grant according to their wisdom.

My point is that petitions skew very strongly in favor of planets. And this is probably not accidental. My own experience is that I have attempted to petition fixed stars, decans, mansions and so forth several times over the years and gotten no results at all. (Even Alkaid, which proved especially frustrating to me as you might imagine.)

Picatrix says that when working with stars and planets in tandem, one chooses stars for durability and planets for agility and speed. I think this is the key to why petitions favor planets.

When we petition we generally want something granted in relative haste. If we petition Jupiter for wealth, we want money to pay our debts and elevate our social class and luxuries–we don't make that petition for our grandchildren to be tycoons. When we petition Mars to inflict harm upon our enemies, we want them punished in the short term, not to have their graves desecrated in a few decades. And so forth. It seems to me that if we were to petition anything other than a planet, we might get what we ask for, but in a manner both subtle and tardy and as such unsatisfactorily.

Another factor which favors planets is that unlike all other celestial hierarchies, they are the closest to human experience. So much so that they are often incorrectly described as archetypical. (Mercury is both wisdom and folly, because planets are by nature changeable and thus disqualifies them as archetypes.) Each planet rules over a mental state and a type of social role or career; the Sun is embodied in secular leadership, Mercury is embodied in scholars and bankers, and so on. This is why we can petition by aim or by type of person, and we cannot consistently do this for a fixed star, constellation, decan or mansion.

This comes down to, in my opinion, a recognition that not everything which can be made into a talisman is suitable for a petition. This is self-evident when you go down the list of types of talismans in the literature, and you realize that many make little sense to address for favors. For example, an ibn Qurra style talisman which is House based would be difficult to transform into a petition because it's pretty hard to identify which celestial force is actually dominant in its creation.

When you make a petition, it mimics the medieval feudal practices of approaching a prince and begging a boon in exchange for fealty and a service. It's quite clear from the structure of the petition incantations that this is what's going on.

That would be vaguely like being dubbed a knight in the court of a king. You would be given a degree of power, and in exchange be required to look after your liege's interests and be at the ready for his call to war. Since the planetary hierarchies (you may now wish to think of them as medieval courts of seven kingdoms) don't actually wage war with each other per se, by doing a petition you are taking on the responsibility of promoting your liege's interests and defending their honor.

So, how does one do that with the Royal Court of Venus? By dressing in silk and sexy clothes, being flirtatious, having lots of sex, singing songs, and eating sweets. And also encouraging this with others. Not exactly a hard job, if you ask me. But since that's the sort of thing you're asking the Ruler of the Kingdom of Venus for in the first place, there's almost no line at all between having your boon granted and doing your service for your liege.

You expand your leige's domain thereby. You carry his or her banner and sometimes literally wear their signet ring. You become their willing representative and embodiment in the Sublunar Realm. You become living proof of your patron's power and authority. That's what they get out of it. Influence and respect.

This also makes sense in terms of energy and mathematics. If one chooses to think of astrological powers as rays and flows of energy, we know (as the ancients did) that light and sound vibrate according to distinct mathematical frequencies.

Furthermore, they knew that the seven planets and their movements had distinctive mathematical relationships to notes on a musical scale; from which we get the notion of the Music of the Spheres.

By performing a petition, you are attempting to get your muffled inertia-burdened vibratory frequencies to harmonize better with those of that planetary frequency. By doing this, you become a better conduit of that tone, or ray of astral light. Or spirit hierarchy, as I prefer to think of it.

(Where this model has a limitation, however slightly, is that one can do this with several frequencies in alternation rather than just one inflexibly.)

It's sometimes hard to adapt to the notion that spirits might also be energies, etc. But this is a very old idea. Pythagoras felt that numbers and ratios were gods, or were beings that the gods themselves served.

In the realm of optics, Al Kindi felt that spirits were all rays: They were made of different kinds of energy, and vibrating at different mathematical frequencies. The interactions of these vibrations were what created Time in the first place.

It all connects together.

Elections Don't Make Talismans, But Forms Do

Elections do not make anything magical. Electional astrology has existed quite independently from magic. Traditional electional texts include detailed formulas for getting a haircut, getting married, going on a journey, starting a war, or preparing a feast. That does not mean the haircut is magical. Your ham and cheese sandwich is not magical. Your marriage vows may feel magic, but come the divorce you will be utterly and appropriately disenchanted. (In case you were wondering, the appropriate consolation gift for a recently divorced person is a lemon cake. They married a complete lemon– and definitely need a nice treat after all of that.)

Elections do not make anything into a talisman. If you mix Mercurial herbs into a perfume during a Mercury election, it is not and cannot be a talisman. It *might* be magical, but if you asked people in the 1400s most people would say NO. If you asked whether it was a talisman, *everyone* would say NO. If you believe otherwise, you have missed some very important aspects of your education in the world of Astrological Magic.

The reason why most people would have considered a Mercury perfume to be non-magical is that they would have actually considered this a medicine. Doctors who were making such things usually did not consider these sorts of things magical, nor did religious authorities. This includes those who approved of magic, despised magic, and even those who disbelieved in magic entirely.

Even if you did consider this magical, the reason why this could never be considered a talisman is because there's no *image*. When you mixed up a bunch of herbs and put it into a liquid, it doesn't coalesce into the form of a man with winged sandals, a frog, or any of the other Forms which connect to the power of Mercury and draw the spirit into matter.

You may have heard that the Western branch of this tradition was called Scholastic Image Magic. This is a subcategory of *image magic*. Images are talismans. If there's no image, it can't be a talisman. Image = talisman. Everyone should know this. Our canonical texts refer to talismans as image far more often than as, uh, talismans. That should be a hint that we should understand how people in the ancient world understand what an image (in both a narrow and broad sense) was and how it worked.

The entirety of the theory of this magic is based on a mix of the Theories of Forms created by Plato and Aristotle: When you look at a cloud that looks like a fish, or a stone engraved like a fish, or an actual fish, your recognition isn't happening in your brain but is a *cosmic event*. In Plato's formulation, it connects your intellect with the supercelestial World of Forms. And that connection is of such enormous power that using it correctly can completely transform reality.

People neglect this to their misfortune. Plato described the location of the World of Forms as "hyperouranos" which means above the heavens. Many consider this a mere metaphor, but to the cosmology we depend upon in magic it's a huge deal. It means we know where it lives, and if we know where it lives we can *manipulate* it.

The Forms are in the same realm as the gods or God. Images tap into Forms.

Images, therefore, have powers closely akin to gods.

Forms are so powerful that when something takes part of their power in the Sublunar Realm, part of their sublime essence is poured into it. However, if the right material becomes an image *at the right moment* i.e. an election, that essence is strong enough to do something which almost never happens: It carries a celestial spirit down into our physical universe and embeds it into hard matter. It is as peculiar a transformation as getting a fish to breathe air and fly–but when propelled by divine force, it is possible.

And yes, the matter has to be hard or the ability for the spirit to root in it is so meager that it will be brief or entirely impossible. Like attracts like, and celestial beings are unchanging and so it will thrive in materials which have minimal capacity for change (a diamond) as opposed to materials which are wholly unstable (a liquid.) Furthermore, anything which is not solid at all has no capacity to have an image. Try drawing a portrait of someone in water.

You *can* even create a talisman without an election, but it will require an image. It just won't be terribly powerful. Just read lapidary texts and you'll see this all the time. A nazar (the Turkish blue eye amulet) is arguably a very *very* weak Solar talisman.

Furthermore, images are pictorial. When you see a Pisces talisman and it's two fish on it, you probably can tell it's got something to do with those animals that swim. If you see a charm with the *word* FISH on it and you don't read English at all, you probably won't think of anything aquatic. That's why objects made up of words and no pictures at all cannot be talismans. The capacity for universal *recognition* is the fuel which embeds the celestial spirit into matter. (It should also be noted that it's the capacity for recognition which is the requirement, not the actual recognition. If recognition were required, messily made talismans and those which were concealed would not work.)

Objects of power do exist which are almost entirely words. Solomonic Pentacles are a great example; with only a few exceptions they are words and geometrical figures. But they are not talismans of any sort. They are not depending upon the World of Forms. They certainly can be elected, but they still won't be talismans. Objects whose power use words exclusively are rarely tapping into the power of celestial entities, because they respond less well to words than to images. *Picatrix* and *De Radiis* say that words are very important, but as augmentative elements rather than the sources of power.

The Divine proximity of Forms implies that the process of creating celestial images (talismans) is probably more powerful than celestial powers alone. Some would say that this extreme divine power is expended in forcing a celestial entity to descend into an alien realm and take up a material body. Others would say that this extreme divine power is also used to give talismans the ability to warp fate by divine mandate.

And that is why talismans are so interesting. The best argument for talismans being able to override nativities is their intimate connection with Forms and by proxy Divine supremacy.

None of this is happening or can happen when you elect a tincture or some other thing.

There are other objects which may be sold or passed off as talismans, but which have care needs or conditions that are decidedly not that of an authentic talisman. *If your talisman needs frequent care, it's probably not actually a talisman.* It's some other kind of magical object, like an amulet, charm, or vessel. If it *is* an amulet, charm or vessel, it generally needs to be fed or prayed over periodically in order for it to work. Amulets, charms and vessels do not require complex elections, and it's unclear if they benefit from them at all.

I use amulets, charms and vessels all the time. They have their values, though talismans are stronger. A serious practitioner will use many types of magical objects and recognize their differences. The only difference between a $250 talisman that you need to reconsecrate and a $2 lucky rabbit's foot which needs to be prayed over with Psalm 23 and dressed with Van Van Oil... is *the price tag.* They basically do the same thing, and work just as efficiently. One just looks fancier than the other.

Just for the record, I do use Jewish folk and Kabbalistic charms from time to time, and I do not elect these. They don't seem to help or hurt them. I also use Solomonic Pentacles, and while electing them *as* talismans can enhance their potency, they aren't fundamentally talismans. I've made them at completely random times and had legendary successes there.

Unlike other artifacts created within other practices,, note that we are not "consecrating" our talismas. While the use of the term "consecration" is widespread within occult texts, the astute will notice that I employ it minimally. This is because it means totally different things to different practitioners.

With most contexts, "consecration" means rendering something sacred. Albertus Magnus would have said this was impossible, because talismans are not holy but natural constructs.

The main use of this appears to be the construction of the talisman: At the point when it is ensouled, a celestial entity which may or may not be an angel enters the matter. Or the natural virtues do. The prayers and incantations and suffumigations certainly have a role, but the timing is generally accepted to be when the object enters its final form. But some people mean just the prayers, which makes me wonder when they're doing what, and where they got that idea from.

Finally, some people are calling consecration the ritualized process of transfer from the creator to the master/owner. Chris Warnock used to call this attunement and I still do, for want of a better term. It makes me a little squirmy because not everybody sees talismans as having religious qualities (Albertus) and this is not actually when the talisman becomes sacred, if it ever does–that's when it's ensouled.

The key to understanding magic is *identifying where the power comes from.* If it's not using Forms, there's no reason to suspect it would do anything interesting except optimize its effects. That's why the perfume election isn't supposed to do anything other than smell extra nice. Celestial influence just makes it do its job better, not give it extra capabilities. You need a Form for that.

When we make a talisman in Scholastic Image Magic, we use elections in place of routine maintenance. The source of power is the timing, thus celestial forces– not the magician channeling the divine or using their own vital force. A well-made talisman emanates power continuously, and does not need to consume attention or offerings or power. They are like the Sun; they emit energy and consume nothing in return. Canonical texts do not suggest talismans require any routine maintenance. Canonical texts do not suggest that the lifespan of a talisman can be extended except by making it from superior materials in the first place.

Celestial power embedded in a well-made talisman is eternal, though the link to the Sublunar tends to fade after a time ranging from a couple of decades to a couple of millennia. It's not clear that this lifespan of sorts can be extended at all.

In fact, a shortcut to getting amulets, charms, and vessels to work *without* prayer, offerings, or feedings is to place them with a talisman. The talisman is actually a more efficient source of power for them than your own personal energy or channeled power.

Talismans are massive labor-savers, but when they behave in a manner which is foreign to the tradition it's an indication that something has gone wrong. It could be that it's a low-power object like a charm with a high price tag instead, or something riskier.

Another possibility when your talisman is requiring service in order to function is that it is a vampiric talisman. I believe that when L1 is afflicted and the significator is on the MC, the talisman will operate, but drain the dignity of the user. One way this drain may manifest is requiring labor to function. Another is that it will make the user sick and unlucky in broad ways. And yet another is that unless labor is volunteered, the talisman will feed on the user as a substitute. Vampiric talismans can be used in the short term, but should probably be destroyed.

Yet another possibility is the rare but real problem Albertus Magnus obsessed upon- the talisman is possessed by a devil. Unless you can eject the foreign entity, the whole talisman needs to be destroyed. And you should probably find out how that happened in the first place, because it could recur.

Both vampiric talismans and demonic talismans are uncommon, so don't panic. But I am seeing a lot more charms being sold as "talismans" and customers wondering why the results are so meager especially with all the offerings they're giving.

Some talismanic spirits enjoy attention and work better when treated certain ways, but they do not require it. I anoint my rings with spiritual perfumes daily; usually Hoyt's Cologne with herbs in it. I used to anoint them with fragrance oils keyed to their affinities, but rapidly discovered this was a completely wasted effort, both costly and messy. I do this anointing as a reward for their extra services to me. If talismans were cats, this would be catnip not tuna. It's a treat. They don't actually starve if you don't feed them.

The pendants I wear around my neck and the talismans in my pockets generally get no attention at all, and function well. Talismans empower *you*-you don't empower *them*.

How Does a Talisman Work?

Talismans of this tradition do not last forever, though they can last a very long time. Their longevity has nothing to do with their maintenance or feeding or any ritual activity, however.

The lifespan of talismans is subject to two factors; the materials they are made of, and the type of celestial entity inhabiting it.

Most of our material on these issues come from *Picatrix* and Ficino. They agree on most matters but differ on some rationales and minutiae.

Two passages in *Picatrix* distinguish the longevity of talismans by type of celestial entity or force. The first is when *Picatrix* states that a talisman to bless or curse a home should be made of a planetary talisman, but a talisman made to bless or curse a city should be made from a fixed star.

This is meaningful when you realize that in most traditional cultures, homes were not made of stone but of wood, thatch, and clay, and would gradually become infested with vermin. The result of this was that communities would raze every home and rebuild it every twenty to forty years for the sake of hygiene. That should be the approximate lifespan of a planetary talisman.

Cities, by contrast, could last thousands of years. The implication here is that fixed star talismans last much longer.

Elsewhere, *Picatrix* says that it is best to elect talismans with planets conjoined with compatible fixed stars. In this way the vigor of the planet will be added to the durability of the fixed star. The implication here is that planetary talismans are not as enduring as fixed stars, and fixed star talismans do not have the vigor of planetary talismans.

In yet another location *Picatrix* says that the powers of the fixed stars are enduring because they do not exhibit retrogradation. This is, we understand, that they exist at the upper levels of the visible universe and take part in many of the traits of the true eternity of the 9th Sphere- but also because they are orderly in character, unlike disobedient retrograde planets.

There are two more things we can derive from this.

Firstly, spirits of celestial spheres often behave similar to those which are proximal to them. If the fixed star talismans are durable in a manner similar to those of the Zodiac and Faces, then the talismans of the uppermost planets should be among the longest lasting of the bunch. Which makes sense, because Saturn and to some degree Jupiter are associated with longevity.

Secondly, we can derive another revelation. If part of why the fixed star talismans are durable is because they do not exhibit retrogradation, there are other things which also do not reverse course- the Luminaries are never retrograde. This suggests that talismans of the Luminaries might also be long lasting in the same way as fixed star talismans, Saturn and Jupiter.

This ultimately leads us to speculate that Mars, Venus and Mercury talismans are the talismans which need to be replaced every couple of decades; though the longevity of Luminary talismans is more speculative.

Another factor which reinforces the above are several references to planetary speed in *Picatrix*, suggesting that planets moving faster than average will have more palpable effects, and planets moving slower than average will either have subtle effects or even completely fail.

There are hints that talismans which act quickly burn out faster, and talismans which work slowly provide more profound and durable effects. But this has as much to do with materials as the elections.

Picatrix is narrower in its statements about the relationship between talismanic longevity and materials. It makes a point that while talismans made of wood are legitimate (and in the Latin *Picatrix* provides a fig wood example in the Plinian Lunar Mansion section), they do not last long because wood decays.

What *Picatrix* is trying to say here is that materials which are subject to the primary traits of the Sublunar Sphere, generation and corruption, are alien to the eternal nature of celestial entities and thus provide poor bodies for them, which they abhor and seek to escape from quickly.

Eternal beings find matter related to generation and corruption to be very unpleasant and are even willing to "die" to escape them. This is less so with wood, which lasts a relatively long time, but is moreso with waxes (which can be made into short-lived secondary talismans), food and drink (which can also be made into secondary talismans), and contact with sexual fluids and bodily waste–which are enough to enrage celestial entities of any and all types. In my experience sex and visits to the restroom both need to be handled with care when wearing talismans.

Ficino is a bit more specific and thought-provoking. He was far narrower about the materials talismans could be made from; only gemstones, gold and silver were suitable materials because they contained quintessence. Herbs could also contain quintessence, but not of the type that they could be made into proper talismans.

Even within this range of options, Ficino believed that soft gemstones behaved quite differently than hard gemstones. Softer gemstones released astral light faster and burned out more quickly, but harder gemstones emitted astral light more slowly and could last many more years. And he didn't mean wear-and-tear, but a fundamental principle.

Hard gemstones like diamonds and rubies and sapphires are very resistant to change, which is expressed in how difficult it is for them to be cut, engraved, or broken. This is seen as an analogy to how the stars themselves are- they are eternal and do not change. But shiny, twinkling gemstones are the closest analogues to stars that we find here on Earth. Their shining beauty and resistance to generation and corruption or change makes hard gemstones irresistible as bodies for celestial spirits because they feel familiar; they feel like home.

Spirits in soft gemstones want to fulfill their duties quickly and return to the heavens relatively soon, but spirits in hard gemstones find their sojourn in our world to be very comfortable so they work slowly and meticulously and are reluctant to depart prematurely.

This might lead you to believe that everyone should always use hard gemstones and fixed stars or naturally slow planets. That would be an error.

Everyone should have some of these in their arsenals for certain, but a lot of the time we need our magic to work quickly and manifest in a spectacular manner. That's what soft materials and faster planets are good for, even if that means they may need to be replaced at some point.

In my own practice I often pair two talismans of the same planet in different dignities, but also in different stones: one soft and one hard, to get the best effects of all kinds.

Materials aside; I tend to think Venus, Mars, Mercury and possibly the Sun and Moon talismans will need to be replaced periodically. My guess is that your Venus and Mercury talismans will need to be replaced twice in your lifetime and possibly the Moon, Mars and possibly the Sun once. Your Jupiter and Saturn talismans will outlast your lifespan as will your fixed star talismans. It's not clear what this means for other classes of talismans like Faces and Lunar Mansions.

But all of that can be modified by materials and other factors- so I expect my Venus DoE talismans to last a very long time because they're in the DoE and that's a very special configuration, and I expect my iron pyrite Mercury talismans to last a very long time because they're mostly made of iron which is very hard and hard gemstones last longer. I think there's a passage in Ficino which says that gold is so temperate that it can be alloyed with no meaningful diminution of power, and the same is probably true of silver. I use sterling silver exclusively.

But to reiterate, none of this involves maintaining rituals or offerings or any other thing with your talismans. I doubt any of that can extend their lifespans to any appreciable degree, any more than petting your dog every day will help it to live to ninety. The lifespan of a talisman is a natural process which cannot be modified much once it has been initiated.

Even if they want to stay, they cannot. This world was not meant for them.

But that does not mean their spirits dissipate; they are eternal beings. They cannot be destroyed. They just need to go back home at the appointed time. Chances are, they'll be back down here someday.

Page 38 of the *Picatrix* states: "Similarly, a feeble disposition revealing itself in an otherwise strong place is the proper disposition for things out of which images are made; for everything is disposed to receive whatever work corresponds to it. This is a foundation of this work, and all accords with it. When something is disposed to receive an influence, the reception will take place; and when the reception has taken place, the effect will be open and manifest, and the figure receives strength. The effect will be as you desire insofar as the matter and the form are conjoined into unity, the way the figure of a man is united with a mirror or water, or as the unity of spirit and body."

Effectively what I believe this passage to be saying is that if the working is orderly and consistent with the representations and affinities of the objective you seek, and the only weak link in the chain is your ease at obtaining that objective by mundane means, that weak link will mend because it will fall in line with the magical activity.

If everything is strong, there is no problem and thus no need for a talisman. Talismans are most effective when the one single thing which doesn't fit the pattern is your problem. The stars are in optimal positions, the suffumigations and sigils are just right, sacrifices performed to perfection- and the imperfect part which corresponds to them in this Sublunar world, easily becomes perfected and wholly as you wish.

So, if your bank account is empty and you perform a supremely perfect money talisman or petition with the ideal suffumigations for money, the proper election for money, the correct evocation for money, the most unambiguous image for money, your finances will incline to conform with everything else listed and your money will manifest. The material world has a strong tendency to conform with consistent spiritual arrangements that you make on every other level.

What's key here is the use of "reception." Much like two or more planets in reception help each other out to achieve a goal, when a talisman is made the aim is to get every component of the working in sync so that it will help the weak factor get a leg up. The weak factor in this case is whatever challenge you are seeking to overcome.

Consistency tends to create further consistency; and if you line up everything else to create a clear pattern, the final pieces which are out of place will tend to order themselves as they are supposed to be. The last piece of any jigsaw puzzle is the easiest to solve. Consistency of work in many things naturally subjugates the one thing which deviates from it. This is because of cosmic eros, and the tendency of things to create a unity out of what initially is of mixed nature and conflicting affinities.

Picatrix Rubeus page 250:

"When images are fashioned in this way, they will be lasting and complete in their effects, and if they are not fashioned in this way, their effects will be destroyed by the destruction of their terrestrial material and the destruction of the composition thereof. Durability comes from the fixed stars, but images have a better nature and a better effect when they are made with the planets, and the effects are more durable when a planet aspects a fortune, which augments the same with the strength and potency it draws to Earth from the heavens."

There continues to be some ambiguity between durability of talisman and durability of effect.

However, what is revealed here is that a harmoniously constructed talisman will produce permanent effects, whereas a less perfect talisman's effects will end when the talisman itself is destroyed.

"By sages, magical images are called talismans, which may be translated 'violators,' because whoever makes an image does so by violence, and makes it by conquering the substance of which it is made. To work victoriously he makes it with mathematical proportions and influences, and uses celestial writing. These images are made *from their proper substances in order that they might receive the aforementioned influence,* and this is done at appropriate times. By suffumigations they are strengthened, and spirits are drawn into these images." *- Picatrix* I:2

I highlight the passage which says that materials of the talisman must be optimal in order to receive a celestial influence. This is important for two reasons.

Firstly, it emphasizes the materiality of talismans very early in the book and seems to give materials almost equal importance as elections.

Secondly, the implication is that while some materials receive desirable celestial influences best, other materials resist reception of undesirable celestial influences. This principle can be applied more broadly, beyond talismans into people places and things, and opening the door to the *Picatrix* notions of Remediation.

It's also important in that this is one of the first instances where *Picatrix* uses the word "reception" idiosyncratically, to describe the variable capacity of anything to be influenced by a specific celestial force. Colleagues have described this as a bottleneck principle. We expand that bottleneck to maximize the potency of talismans, but narrow the bottleneck to prevent undesirable influences.

Reducing the opportunities for an afflicted planet to influence a person, place or thing is what I call Diminution. It is an effective method of remediation which is based in magical theory but does not require talismans or rituals.

"Magic is divided into two parts, that is, theoretical and practical. The theoretical part is knowledge of the places of the fixed stars, because from these are composed the celestial figures and forms of the heavens, and of how their rays project into the planets that move of themselves, and of understanding figures of the heavens when they wish to make them. In this is included all that the sages of old have said about the elections of hours and times to work with images. You should know that those who have equaled the ancients in making images know that the virtue of images consists wholly in the election of hours and times of the proper constellations, and in appropriate substances from which the images are made.

"Words also form a part of magic, because words themselves have magical virtues. Plato says the same thing, that just as a friend can become an enemy through wicked and insulting words, good and friendly words can turn an enemy into a friend. By this it is clear that words have magical power in them. The greatest strength is achieved when several strengths are joined together to overcome, and this is the perfect virtue in magic. This comprises the theoretical part." - *Picatrix* I:2

Picatrix here says that the virtue of talismans is *wholly* from elections and materials, but the strength can be augmented with additional factors. Verbal components are one, and elsewhere it says suffumigations are another. *Picatrix* advises we augment our talismans with every possible means of strength. And this turns virtue, to strengths, and finally to the perfection of the virtue.

Here's where we get the conflict with Albertus Magnus, asking us to strip away incantations and suffumigations–the exact things which make talismans stronger. But the essence of talismans is down to two fundamental factors: the *timing* and the *materials*. Both should be optimal.

Animal, vegetable, and mineral: The threefold circuit is what completes magic. This is true in Hoodoo as well in the construction of mojo bags.

Scholastic magical images tend to elicit amity among those similar to those depicted.

My 2nd Face of Libra talisman has produced this odd effect of making people with dark skin like and trust me—I've noticed it from the very start. "There rises in the second face of Libra a black man, a bridegroom having a joyous journey. This is a face of tranquility, joy, abundance and good living." I've also suspected that it helps with concord among fellow travelers and newlyweds, but I cannot be as confident. This has also been noted with other Face talismans.

I have observed that my Saturn talisman makes people intimidated by me (which it is supposed to do, as it protects the wearer) with the exception of people with very strong natal Saturns, in which case they find me fascinating and very pleasing. I suspect this principle applies to other talismans and nativities, including fixed stars on the natal Ascendant.

Yet now I have a new discovery. With Lunar Mansion talismans whose purpose is to attract respect, love, or friendship, the shade of the stone used keys to the skin tone (and hair color to a much lesser degree) of the subject. People with pale skin respond most to the quartz talismans, the darkest skin to the onyx talismans, and intermediate skin tones resonate best with iron pyrite. Don't ask me what lapis lazuli, silver, or moonstone Mansion talismans do; I haven't tried those.

Now, some of this applies to Face talismans as well. I used a yellow agate for a 2nd Face of Cancer talisman, and promptly got groped randomly by a beautiful Asian woman wandering the West

Village in a state of extreme intoxication. (It was weird as hell, but not unpleasant.)

In Hoodoo, petition papers are often colored according to the skin tone of the subject; brown bag paper for African-American subjects and white paper for Caucasian subjects. Some of this logic does seem to apply in stone choice, though I confess that this whole racial element makes me squirm a bit.

If your money magic isn't working, stop playing video games where you accumulate treasure or even points.

The spiritual powers which you have called upon rarely can distinguish between the virtual cash in a game and the virtual cash in your bank account, and they will almost invariably work on whatever is easier to manifest. It's all just bytes in a computer today, after all.

I found this out some years ago when goofing off in a game where I accumulated a conspicuous amount of treasure, even while my real life finances were stagnant. And part of the reason I was gaming was that it was an inexpensive way to pass the time and relieve stress about money!

It took me a while to realize that my ring of Deneb Algedi was working on the game rather than what I actually needed. When I stopped playing, my finances began to improve.

I recently met with a fellow maker of talismans. He made a point of drawing my attention to the fact that he was not wearing any talismans at all. When I asked why, he said that he felt that wearing them was "provocative." I found this very puzzling. If you make talismans and you aren't wearing your own merch at all, it looks to me that you are ashamed of your creations–that they are defective in some way. I know that I wouldn't buy something from a person who wouldn't use it for themselves.

While it varies a bit by tradition, the general concept of a sorcerer or magician is that they are a master of spirits. The more powerful the spirit, the more powerful the mage. The more spirits in their employ, the more powerful the mage as well. This is an idea which is so fundamental that it is the default assumption in indigenous "shamanic" practices all over the world. A magician is never a singular being, but the visible head of countless armies of entities.

Talismans of the Scholastic Image Magic tradition are physical bodies for quasi-angelic beings which are used for any number of tasks. They tend to be more visible signs of spirit employment than other traditions, though if you study indigenous traditions many spirit workers carry bottles and bones and parchment and tassels for the same purposes.

I do realize that wearing a lot of jewelry on a man in Eurocentric cultures looks peculiar, but personally I think the tradeoff is worth it. A shaman wearing a vest with hundreds of knots for bound spirits also looks weird in their cultures, but nobody is making a fuss about that. Power is inherently weird, and weirdness is itself a kind of power. Embrace it.

A magician without such items isn't actually disarmed, unless they are complete fools. They're just employing spirits in ways a little less obvious. While many of those entities can be benevolent, a lot of them are wild or parasitic. Talismanic spirits are a lot safer when well-constructed–and far easier to get rid of when something goes wrong. (Because being a sorcerer is never a safe pursuit.)

That considered, when I encounter a magician without any clue to what they might be using, I don't actually feel safe. I don't assume they're disarmed. Instead, I wonder if they might be unstable and that their servants aren't fully under their control. Because you see a lot of that out there. After all, I'm the guy people call to clean up messes when that kind of relationship goes wrong.

And yes, I use countless spirits which aren't bound to talismans as well. That's the output of my work in the 80s and 90s, long before I believed in astrology or heard about this tradition. I just think the spirits employed by Scholastic Image Magic can do many things that the others cannot.

I also wonder what he meant by "provocative." Do people think that someone wearing visible talismans will cause them to become mind-controlled zombies? Honestly it doesn't actually work that way–and besides, you don't need talismans for that kind of influence if that were desired. There are many ways to influence the minds of others, both magical and mundane. Only a small portion of that has anything to do with talismans.

People sometimes ask me if there is any such thing as too much power when they see my rings. What do I need all of that for, anyway? There's an aphorism which comes to mind- you can never be too rich or too thin. But that's not a great analogy, because a person can probably be too rich or too thin (though I think many of us wish we had the "too rich" sort of problem rather than the other way around). I am considered powerful, but my goals are far more ambitious than those of my peers. My needs are also probably different than yours, as are the needs of virtually anybody, ultimately. Even if your goals are conventional and your needs fulfilled, do you really want to make a choice between wealth or health or love or knowledge or freedom? If you just want one of those things and are only wearing a single talisman as a result, I'm glad you're content.

Still, I think that people like that lack ambition. Ambition is one of the fundamental ingredients in a competent practitioner. In order to seize the fires of heaven, you have to be bold enough to try. I tend to think that passive people make very bad magicians.

But occasionally I do encounter a naked magician; a person who has the capacity for power yet is afraid of using it. I feel sorry for them. But if magic is a finite resource, that just means there's more for the rest of us.

The Ideal Talisman

Awareness of another person's magical operations, particularly with regard to the preparation of talismans, dampens their effects and often nullifies them completely. Not everyone believes this, but I'm not alone in this opinion either. There are admonitions of secrecy in the grimoire texts and even indications among contemporary practitioners which suggest this further.

I'm very happy to share information about elections after the fact, or discuss talismans, or discuss matters in a general way. I'm also open to providing valid elections that I have no intention of using.

Some grimoires prohibit disclosure of arcana to the profane for a variety of reasons. My own experience is that if a non-participant becomes aware of an upcoming magical working- particularly talismanic creation- the talisman loses all potency. There's certainly leeway when it comes to what can be disclosed- but once a person can clearly visualize the election, either the purpose or the timing, it's kaput. If the non-participant can visualize only part of the purpose or timing, it's somewhat safe. Once the ritual or talisman is created, it's rooted into reality and can't be harmed by mere awareness.

It has been argued that this is precisely the opposite to what famed occultist Aleister Crowley suggests about his particular version of magic(k). It's my opinion that Crowley was a complete charlatan. In the 1990s I developed a suspicion- something that didn't make sense about his outlook, so I devised an experiment. I codified his perspectives on magic, and decided to apply the exact opposite of Crowley's teachings in every way. The result was that my ability to achieve magical effects substantially improved.

I don't have a problem with many of the Golden Dawn folk- they were just operating in a wholly new spiritual technology which appropriated a lot of the imagery of older forms. It works too, it just doesn't work at all like the talismanic-astrological tradition.

I single out Crowley as being a charlatan, because his unique contributions to that new tradition of magic are ineffective and even downright destructive. A lot of people get into magic and gravitate to Crowley, assuming he was the number one authority. Most of then conclude magic is rubbish after futzing around with MiT&P for a few months. Magic isn't the dud, only Crowley.

A question I get asked a lot is when is the critical electional window for a talisman. Is it when you craft the talisman? Buy the materials? Say the incantation? Give it to the recipient? I find this puzzling because Christopher Warnock sleuthed this out about thirty years ago, and it's been an essential foundation of this revival. How can someone have any real knowledge of Astrological Magic and not know the key factor which makes it all work?

Chris deduced from our canonical texts that the talisman must take its *final form* during the *electional window*. Everything we've been doing for decades now has been based on this understanding.

Now, it's possible that the necessity to attain the final form during the electional window is incorrect. But if it is incorrect, it profoundly undermines the rationale for the overwhelming majority of talismans which have been made during the revival (and probably in centuries past as well.)

That is why I consider the idea of liquid talismans to be so problematic. They greatly undermine the whole theoretical basis of Astrological Magic.

The good news is that if we accept that solid and liquid mixtures can be made powerful by elections (even arguably magical) without being understood as talismans, there is no conflict at all. Things get complicated when you introduce the concept of non-solid magical creations *as talismans*, because they can never actually take a final form.

If we study the canon of electional astrology, different types of elections have unique rules about the critical moment. If it's not a talisman, it doesn't need to attain final form-the critical period could be when all the ingredients are fully added, or even when the first ingredient is placed in the mixing vessel. It still may be powerful, and it certainly could be called magical. But it's not the same thing.

In any case, if what we are doing has a fundamental logic to it rather than just deflecting the inconsistencies as "well, it's just magic, of course" then we have to reject the pandering to the irrational and make definitions and distinctions.

I think and always have believed that reasoning through all of this is productive and will incite progress in our endeavors.

One of the things we actually don't have a lot of knowledge regarding is the cumulative effect of wearing many different types of talismans at once. My contention is that it is safer to use a talisman whose principal star is on the Midheaven, but whose Ascendant is afflicted, if this is just one of several talismans whose Ascendants are quite strong and fortified. This is partially why I advise the use of talismans with afflicted Ascendants for short term effects. The other reason is that it's sometimes appropriate to use a talisman which makes the wearer unattractive, irritable, and ill temporarily if the main goal is critical.

One of the matters *Picatrix* and other sources disclose is that the radiation of talismans when properly made are so strong they overwrite the reality of all receptive substances in their proximity, fading gradually outward. Many of those substances–which can include people–will have nativities with afflicted Ascendants. Yet it is the very nature of talismans to overcome these faults and make them akin to the talismans.

What this means is that under most circumstances, a talisman with a strong essential dignity on a House will overcome the accidental and essential debilities of the same House of anything it encounters, even if the quantifiable number of the dignities and debilities approach zero when combined. Strength beats an equivalent amount of weakness–it does not neutralize it.

So, though I believe it's best to have talismans without any weak Ascendants, there is a Traditional rationale for using a weak Ascendant talisman for a magus in a hurry.

This is a bit technical, but aspects and conjunctions between planets and aspects and conjunctions with Angles such as the Ascendant behave differently. There is less consensus about the latter. Of all the Angles the Ascendant is the most powerful and most sensitive.

Page 64, *Picatrix Rubeus*: "Next you should learn that they do not calculate these figures in any way except from the nature of the stars and signs. In this way you will be able to understand what was said above concerning the second Face [Decan]. All their sayings are of this sort. What I have said up to this point, you will be able to understand by using your senses and your imagination, and thus you will be able to make all things according to your wishes.

"Abenoaxie... named the watery triplicity, and wrote there... When someone seems to speak of water, a river, a swamp, or any other thing similar to them, you ought to understand that its work is in water. In the same way, all the other figures of the triplicities that are assigned to fire, earth, or air, should be understood in the same way...

"This is what they said about the names of the degrees, and they also said the same thing when they gave examples of their forms in their places, because all these are signs by which you will be able to understand the powers and workings of the degrees. Thus you ought to interpret them in the same way.

"As an example of the foregoing, when someone refers to a mutilated head and mutilated hands, he means by this phrase death and weakness and the way of one planet with others, because all these are ways to understand the effects of the planets, and how other bodies are strengthened by them, so that marvels, and the effects of the planets in these bodies, become apparent. In this way you should understand the whole art of magic."

Picatrix is saying here that the images of the Signs and Faces are constructed from interactions between the essential dignities and natures of the the Signs, Triplicities, Faces and Degrees and the properties of the planets traversing them. Likewise, this is a two-way process, whereby identifying how an particular interaction between planets and each other or with a particular set of Zodiacal degrees can be depicted as an image, this can be used to manifest or influence that image's parallel in the material world.

That means Face images which include a mutilated or ugly figure tend to be governed or empowered by an infortune or a highly afflicted planet or other bad interaction. Likewise, if you want to conjure up a horse, you probably will want to work with Sagittarius- or find lost keys with the 2nd Face of Taurus.

This allows us to break out of the rote recipes for rituals and talismans, and allows us to use the panoply of images available to develop ritual projects and talismans, which do not appear in any available text.

Normally in astrological talismanic work, the objective is to make the talismanic materials maximally receptive to the singular force invested into the object. I have come to observe two peculiar exceptions: When the primary stellar force is applying to a tight trine of another compatible planet, the materials can be fused as a hybrid of the two forces. The second is that when the primary stellar force is not the Moon, and the Moon is exceptionally dignified during the electional window, often a greater share of power can be obtained by using materials compatible with both the primary stellar force (PSF) and the Moon.

Some of this of course deserves expansion, because some of the terminology I use here are innovations of mine. For example, Primary Stellar Force would perhaps be Jupiter when creating a Jupiter Ring, and the Moon as it transits the 28th Mansion when making a Ring of Arrexe. This gets a bit more complex when talking about House-Based Talismans. The materials proper to House-Based Talismans are a debated topic.

Now, the first exception was when a Ring election had the Primary Stellar Force making a tight applying trine to a planet. Let's say that this was a Sun Ring and the Sun was making a tight applying trine with Jupiter. In such an election, it would be uncontroversial to use frankincense as fumigation or herbal matrix beneath the ring, but there might be additional advantages to using lignum aloes (agarwood) or gum mastic as these materials are considered receptive to both Sun and Jupiter.

The second exception was when a Ring election was extremely strong, but also was so strong and unafflicted with the Moon that it could conceivably have been altered slightly to prepare a Moon ring instead. In these circumstances, the coloration and attributes of the Moon can be bled into the range of potential materials of the PSF to create something which is a little greater than the sum of its parts. So, this could be ensuring that the ring band was primarily silver in order to invest greater Lunar force, or a herb which was compatible with both PSF and Moon (or fumigation) to attract greater potency into the gem.

In the latter case, the Moon and PSF do not need to be aspecting, because all elections seem to require the participation of the Moon.

This sort of thing can happen when materials have multiple associations; so lapis lazuli is of Saturn, Sun, and Venus alike. You might have been going in the direction of onyx for your Saturn ring, but you find Saturn is making a tight trine to the Sun and thus want to get a little more of that commanding power in your ring.

Lapis is a more delicate material, but it's also relatively inexpensive, so a canny practitioner could easily make one or more backup rings during the electional window in case the first were damaged. Considering that one of the other stones of Saturn is sapphire, you may end up happier and richer with two lapis lazuli Saturn rings than one sapphire Saturn ring.

But ultimately, this is all about power. The timing of an elected ring of this sort and the proper selection of metals, stones, fumigations, and herbal matrices all increase the potency of the resulting ensouled artifact. The ugliest-seeming of rings can sometimes have the most spectacular of effects, and the most beautiful and beguiling rings the most dangerous to the wearer. I've worn both.

Appearances tell you far less than you might suspect; everything is occult, hidden. In plain sight.

Picatrix IV:4, Greer-Warnock translation: "I say to you further that, if the quantity of stone of which an image is composed is large (that is, between an ounce and a pound), the virtue and power of it will be able to reach from the place where it is for a hundred leagues.

"If it contains a combination of things in its figure, however, its nature will have no motion or effect except that which terminates in its own place, though its motion or effect will not be limited to those of its substance or the nature of the bodies that compose it, for spirits have a wider range than those bodies that contain little spirit."

Talismans made from mineral spheres of even medium sizes will project power for 300 miles in all directions.

Talismans which attempt to draw upon the power of more than one celestial hierarchy will be crippled, like a chariot whose horses are running in different directions. They will have some influence in their immediate environment because they are inhabited by a chimerical spirit, but less than a pure spirit and more than the natural virtues of whatever material the talisman is composed of.

On that note, I hereby coin the term "chimerical spirit"; a temporary union of astral spirits from dissimilar celestial hierarchies in a talisman, which being neither fish nor fowl operates with the virtues of neither.

This notion seemingly creates an inherent limitation upon House-based talismans. Which may explain why I have found them ineffective and frustrating.

One issue many have with creating effective talismans is mixing time periods of astrological belief and calculation.

My own philosophy is that we do best by avoiding anachronisms. If we want to replicate the effects of talismans and petitions of the era of *Picatrix*, we should probably do our best to use the techniques the author used as closely as possible. If we want to replicate the effects of talismans and astrological medicines of the era of Ficino and Agrippa, we should use their techniques similarly- which are somewhat different from the former, but comparable.

We can't actually do that with the talismans of the Hellenistic era, because they either never existed or all traces of evidence of how they were made have been lost. We also probably shouldn't do that with Astrological Magic more recent than William Lilly, because the results have been so unimpressive for generations that it has caused the entire tradition to be marginalized and forgotten except by a few scholars.

Part of what has propelled this is the newfound popularity of Hellenistic astrology and the genuine charisma of its most vocal proponents- and the passion of their converts. Hellenistic astrology is great for natal astrology and probably much else, but not for Scholastic Image Magic.

There is no One True Astrology any more than there is a One True Divination Deck. The Thoth Deck does not invalidate the Sola Busca Deck or the Tarot of the Cat People. Practitioners of Vedic Astrology are not cranks; but it's probably better for some things than others.

What complicates our situation here is that there is a lineage of astrological tradition as we trace the development of the Science of

Images, and as such Qurtubi and Ficino were absolutely studying Hellenistic texts while not being Hellenists themselves. It's sometimes hard to figure out except by close reading which ideas from Dorotheus and Ptolemy and Valens were treated skeptically or de-emphasized by magicians, and which were retained.

To give you specific examples, aversion is a concept which *Picatrix* may have used but we are not completely sure because of translation issues. It's almost completely absent during the Renaissance era in the context of magic, but I have found some non-magical electional recipes which seem to derive from it.

Another key concept in Hellenistic astrology is the Doctrine of Sect. It is pretty central, in fact. But by the time of *Picatrix*, Sect is closely associated with polytheism, and the author seems to go out of his way to attack it in various ways. Aside from its use in Essential Dignities, it's basically gone from Renaissance material. If you are trying to avoid anachronisms and produce powerful talismans of the medieval and Renaissance types, you should probably not be using Sect as a major consideration at the very least.

Page 63: "The ascensions of the images of heaven are of two manners, of which one is the 48 forms drawn from the constellations. This is what we see changing according to the rising and setting of the fixed stars, which are changed from sign to sign, and other images of heaven such as the constellations of the Dog, the Bear, the Rooster, and the like. All these images change from sign to sign and from place to place, and do not simply move in accordance with the heavens as a whole. The constellations in the signs of the Zodiac change much more than the others, because in a thousand years they move from face to face."

Picatrix distinguishes the constellations from the Signs and Decans in this and the following section. He's talking about precession and that means he used Tropical Signs although he used constellations for different purposes.

What he means is that there are two general classes of images; one which focuses on the fixed stars, whose attributes are lent in part from the 48 constellations which they comprise, and another which is composed of 36 Faces. The individual stars drift and pass through each Face in a thousand years.

One thing I should note is that there are two sets of Face/Decan images. In *Picatrix* it calls the Western version Faces and the Hindu version Decans, which is a little odd considering the origin of the latter word. There's another section of *Picatrix* which gives the first few images of the Hindu Decans, and they're the same as the Faces. They use the same sequence of Zodiacal images, and likewise the same sequence of Face/Decan images. What varies is where, perhaps, 0 Aries is and which planet rules each Decan/Face.

However, the latter don't work for me, so perhaps they would work if a Sidereal Zodiac was imposed. Nevertheless, he's saying these two manners operate largely independent of each other for the purpose of selecting talismans.

There is an underlying philosophy, so I think he believes they both work, but some magicians focus on one or the other. But both work.

Because Sidereal puts priority on the stars of Aries for orientation, it's putting faith in the stars- even if it's only one star. To people supporting Tropical, the positions of the stars are more disorderly and irrational and thus less significant- even the star at 0 Aries.

The images apply to both, it's just the rulerships and purposes which vary. There are images from other texts, divorced of purpose in many cases. The sigils are also highly abstracted versions of the images in many cases.

It's clear that sometimes Face talismans were paintings, as *Picatrix* lists pigments for them- however I strongly suspect statuary was preferred.

I'm wearing three Decan rings right now. The strongest by far is the one which had the entire pictorial image along with name engraved, and the other two had just the name and sigil. I don't think that's accidental, but it's too late to redo the two. I may make new ones during the next elections for each, with full iconography.

It just requires patience. Some years are fertile for talismans of one type or other, and some for all and some for none.

Do not keep curse talismans in your home for more than a couple of days. Make them only when you have a target in mind and is immediately accessible. They cannot be stored safely. Make them, deploy them, then run away. Far away.

One of the several reasons I began to study this magical tradition was that it promised to provide curses so powerful and deadly that no other form of magic could fully protect the victim. This promise has been kept. That should give a hint that **SIM** curse talismans cannot be treated like other forms of malefic magic. Nobody is tough enough–that's exactly the whole point.

Another thing to consider is that all **SIM** talismans fascinate and mesmerize people to a certain extent. They emit intense astral light that human beings are not used to experiencing, and we are drawn to them. They are also alive and empathic, projecting emotions which help the owner according to their functions.

This is also true with curse talismans, making them addictive and very hard to get rid of after they get their hooks in you. That doesn't take long either, just like *Frodo* and the *One Ring*. Those myths have a real basis. The spirit of a curse talisman will empathically seduce or intimidate or otherwise manipulate so that it stays where the feasting is easy–which is why it's important to get it away from you quickly, and deposited where most appropriate. In some cases that is under the house of your worst enemy, or buried in a graveyard, or dropped to the bottom of the ocean. That's up to you... While the choice is still yours.

Chapter Four

The Construction of Talismans

How A Talisman is Made

Scholastic Image Magic, or SIM for short, arguably focuses upon the creation of talismans; that is, material objects in which a spirit of the heavens is ritually embedded in order to perform works of wonder. *Picatrix*, also known as *Ghayat El-Hakim* in its original Arabic title, is the largest and most detailed example of this tradition of magical texts. While *Picatrix* is a miscellany of magical and esoteric lore, the majority of it can be said to either provide recipes for the creation of astrological talismans or reference materials and theory which support this endeavor.

Picatrix was never intended to contain all the knowledge necessary for the reader to create talismans, evoke spirits, or the many other secrets it offers. The student of the work was expected to be educated in the system of advanced astrology prominent at that time, with a priority towards electional astrology, the choosing of fortunate or unfortunate times to commence an activity or construct or alter an object. Talismans were simply one way to use an astrological election; by embedding the spirit of a fortunate moment of a particular flavor in matter, the luck or power would emit from the talisman even during times which were mediocre or quite adverse.

The student was also expected to be quite versed in the sciences of the era, which depended heavily upon the works of Aristotle and Pliny and the studies of the alchemists. While astrological associations of metals and gemstones and other materials often differ from those the alchemists used, they overlapped sufficiently that in the absence of guidance from canonical texts of astrology and magic, the student would refer to alchemical teachings as a supplement.

Many of these supplemental texts have been lost or are not available in translation. What modern practitioners do is refer to texts which are compatible but later in history and thus more accessible. Cornelius Agrippa's *Three Books of Occult Philosophy* is a great source for such information, and when herb lore becomes relevant so is Nicholas Culpeper's *Herbal*.

Picatrix is often evasive about the diversity of talismanic implementations. There are hints that wooden talismans are possible, but it gives no details regarding their manufacture. Pigments are often associated with stellar configurations, but again there is little information on how they were to be used, since paper and parchment were not thought to be able to absorb power very well.

What is provided are instructions on how to cast talismans out of metals and colored waxes, and to engrave gemstones. When the proper picture or sigil was inscribed or cast on such an object at the elected time, a spirit of one of the seven planetary hierarchies or one of the many more exotic stellar hierarchies would empower the talisman and give it amazing powers. Incantations and burned incense would facilitate the process and strengthen the creation of the talisman, and compatible herbs would either be placed with it or glued to in some manner to magnify or focus the power towards a particular objective.

In recent centuries the concept of correspondence has eclipsed that of affinity, and to modern practitioners the return to the old way of thinking may be jarring. The alchemists had a one-to-one correspondence between the seven traditional planets and metals, with lead corresponding to Saturn, tin to Jupiter, iron to Mars, gold to Sun, copper to Venus, quicksilver to Mercury, and silver to the Moon. Even later in history, singular colors corresponded to the planets as well; black for Saturn, blue for Jupiter and so on. This is alien to the older and more complex astrological tradition.

In Scholastic Image Magic, there are long lists of metals and minerals (not to mention herbs and animal ingredients) associated with each planetary hierarchy. Furthermore, many materials appear on two or more lists for different reasons. Each planetary hierarchy has multiple colors. Lastly, there is no singular material on each list which is most associated with the planet any more than there is one which is the least. Each material has qualities which in some way resemble the function of one or more planetary hierarchy, which can include color, weight, attractiveness, medicinal usage, flavor, folkloric associations, hardness, translucency and much more. This complexity is often jarring to newcomers in this system.

Metallic gold (and minerals like iron pyrite which resemble it) are prized in Scholastic Image Magic.

An example of these complex associations is the metal gold. The yellowish hue and, when polished, its shininess associate it with the Sun. Its inability to tarnish is associated with the Sun's regularity and mathematical associations with the four seasons. Gold is an excellent material for Sun talismans. However, gold is a very heavy material—almost as heavy as lead—and this is why it is associated with Saturn, the planetary hierarchy associated with weight, gravity and things drawn down into the earth. Saturn talismans can be made perfectly well in gold; in some ways it is superior to lead because it is more rigid and less likely to distort when worn or carried. Gold is highly attractive and desired, and so it gains associations with Venus and also is appropriate for her talismans. Gold is also expensive and thereby gains associations with Jupiter, the governor of riches. Gold is also suitable for Jupiter talismans.

The only planets which can't work with gold are Mars, Mercury, and perhaps the Moon.

Lapis lazuli with iron pyrite inclusions is particularly versatile and inexpensive for making talismans.

More overlap appears in one of the most commonly used gemstones, lapis lazuli. A soft, vividly blue gemstone that is frequently flecked with golden iron pyrite inclusions, it is relatively inexpensive and thus is quite popular among contemporary practitioners of **SIM**. Of greater importance, Marsilio Ficino (a Renaissance genius who practiced **SIM** among many other things) observed that softer materials produced talismans which had shorter lifespans but produced magical effects especially rapidly. *Picatrix* uses a slightly different rationale with the same conclusion. Nevertheless, lapis lazuli with pyrite inclusions gains association with Saturn by two routes; the golden appearance of the pyrite hearkens back to metallic gold and its own associations with Saturn, and because of a historical confusion between lapis lazuli and sapphire- both mean "blue stone" in different languages (Latin and Sanskrit) and the latter is more directly associated with Saturn due to its dark color and extreme hardness. (Saturn governs darkly pigmented things and durability.) Lapis lazuli with pyrite inclusions also has affinity with the Sun because of the golden appearance of the flecks of pyrite. Lapis gains association with Venus because of its oceanic blue color, and the Greek myth of Aphrodite emerging from the sea foam. The Moon arguably has the strongest associations with lapis lazuli because of this oceanic connection, and because of the dependency of the tides upon the Lunar cycles. Additionally, by way of lapidary lore, lapis lazuli has the property of diminishing melancholy and grief, and this quality is added to and magnified by the transformation of a lapis lazuli gemstone into a Saturn, Sun, Venus or Lunar talisman, regardless of its other powers.

These are two, slightly extreme examples of how the 1:1 system of correspondence fails in Scholastic Image Magic. In many instances a gemstone or other material will only have associations with one or two celestial hierarchies. But I illustrate this to make a point; materials such as gemstones, metals and herbs are not singular representatives of a celestial hierarchy in each kingdom of matter, but one of a host of materials which a particular astrological spirit hierarchy finds beautiful, interesting, useful, or more real. Everything in the world is ruled over by one or more planetary hierarchies; there's a lot of redundancy down here. And an alternate way to express this if the notion of spirits is undesirable, is that just like different forms of electromagnetic radiation can penetrate metals and flesh and stone to varying degrees based on type, the rays of astral light (which are the spirits themselves) can irradiate all substances to differing degrees. Only those materials which can be fully irradiated by astral power of any particular variety are capable of becoming the vessels of power that are talismans.

There are an abundance of additional factors to consider when selecting gemstones for the purpose of making a particular sort of talisman. Some are metaphysical and some are practical.

Picatrix advises that one may use the system of humours or temperament to attract and repel animals and people of particular constitutions whose images have been engraved on gemstones. A gemstone which is believed to be hot and dry with the talismanic image of a fierce animal like a lion will attract and tame the animal. A gemstone whose constitution is believed to be cold and wet with the same image and stellar configuration would instead repel lions. The same might be applicable to types of people who might appear on a talisman, such as a king or a warrior. Sadly, lists of the elemental associations of gemstones from the era of *Picatrix* do not appear to be available in translation, and some guesswork is necessary.

Gemstones are believed to be the fruits of the Earth, and are natural phenomena. In the outlook of the scientists of the era, plants were a midpoint between the attributes of animals (both grow) and minerals (neither move about). One of the implications of the continuum between animal and mineral is that to an extent, minerals are parts of the living Earth and closer in nature to a living oak tree than a carcass. This explains why gemstones which are in various ways not natural do not make good talismans. Artificial diamonds and rubies, irradiated gems, dyed gems, and sometimes even heated minerals do not absorb the essence of the spirit beings adequately in order to turn them into talismans. Sometimes when they do work, they produce unpleasant side effects. Synthetic gemstones are akin to silk flowers and wax fruit; they may look like the real thing but often are inadequate replacements.

The color of gemstones is a complicated issue. Gemstones of particular colors are indeed associated with particular planetary hierarchies; pretty much any white stone can be used for Jupiter, for example. Nevertheless, this is an instance where an association is very superficial and often will produce an inferior talisman. Gems which have very particular associations with planets because of unique properties take precedence over something like color alone, which is far more general. Many gemstones which are powerfully associated with a particular planet are of extremely counterintuitive colors.

Another issue with color is that on a mineralogical level, several named gemstones are basically the same mineral and differ only by color. In this instance, the differences of color are the source of the identity rather than chemical composition or crystalline structure. One example is onyx, traditionally a black or brown stone with white banding. Onyx can be used for Saturn talismans, Moon talismans, and the fixed star Corvus. Sardonyx is a stone which is red or orange with white or yellow banding. Other than color, there is no difference between the two. However, sardonyx is used for the talismans of the fixed star Antares, and neither the Moon nor Saturn. Antares is a reddish star, whose appearance resembles that of the stone. It is an exception to the rule. A more well known pairing like this is that of sapphire and ruby; both are the mineral corundum, but the former is black or dark blue and the latter red. Their metaphysical associations are completely different. Seeming paradoxes sometimes occur. The emerald is suitable for Jupiter and Mercury talismans—planets which are otherwise completely opposite to each other in every way. It is not enough to understand which materials are associated with one or more planets. Whenever possible, one must understand why.

One more consideration for gemstone talismans that can be of crucial use is that of shape. The most important consideration is practical; you need a gemstone with a large flat surface—large enough to engrave a sigil or, far better, a pictorial image using a diamond stylus. Emerald cut and marquis cut gemstones can provide enough surface for a small sigil but little more. Cabochons, whether hemispherical or ovoid, are the better option. They provide maximal surface area and are portable. They work in ring settings and can even be secreted in a pocket or wallet.

They also have a harmonious shape. Aristotle believed that the cosmos was spherical as the macrocosm, and this was mirrored in all spiritual beings as a microcosm; the shape of all spirits (in spite of appearances) are spheres. Anything which approaches the shape of the sphere, including ovoid shapes, circles and hemispheres, are particularly suitable vessels for a spirit being such as a talismanic entity. So, though it is seldom practical, the optimal talisman is a mineral sphere of the largest manageable size.

The factors which must be taken into account in the selection and preparation of gemstones and other material objects for transformation into talismans in Scholastic Image Magic can be daunting at first. It requires a great deal of specialty knowledge, but the authors of the *Picatrix*, Agrippa and other masters of **SIM** tended to describe talismans made in an optimal way in order to minimize side effects and maximize their power—and massive power it can be indeed. However, the average experimenter (or master of this system in a bit of a hurry) can use inexpensive or even slightly inappropriate timing and materials to create talismans which provide sufficient and immediate results. This is an elite system of magic, but the basics are accessible to all with the drive and determination to ascend.

Page 30: "What the heavens are and what their substance is the shape of heaven is spherical... for this is the shape of spirit, as though saying that spirit is first and nothing in the world is older than it... but the perfect form and figure is the circle, because it is the first of all figures and is made from a single line... Now heaven, as we have said, is a sphere... A circular line surrounds it; in the middle of that circle is a point so positioned that all lines drawn from it to the surrounding circle are of equal length, and this point is called the center. It is said that these lines signify the rays that the stars cast upon the earth, which is at the center. From these come the power and virtue of images... from it all the powers of spirits are summoned."

So what we are seeing here is that circles and spheres are the shape of spirit, and this is why talismans are most frequently in disk or spherical shapes, as this is the optimal repository for housing a spirit.

Another interesting thing being pointed out here is that though the Tropical Zodiac is an attribute of the 9th Sphere, the ecliptic circle still goes beyond this and reaches to the outermost boundary of the cosmos up until the point where only the One exists.

This suggests, perhaps, the initial division of the cosmos from One into subordinate parts is marked by the ecliptic or some analogue of it.

I'm sure square pendant talismans work, but I'd generally tend to prefer an alternative if all other factors were equal. Using circles or spheres are a way of taking the talisman to the next level, but not on the scale of importance of election details or materials or even suffumigations.

Stones and Other Materials

"In this part I intend to reveal how each planet corresponds to metals and stones, and to the figures of the planets and their marvelous operations.

"The first is Saturn. Of the metals Saturn has iron and part of gold, his stones are diamond, onyx, cameo, and azebehe that is black and clear, and iron ore and magnesia and ruby in part, and yellow marcasite, and also hematite.

"Of the metals, Jupiter has lead, and precious stones that are white and golden and part of carnelian and emerald and quartz and crystal and all stones that are white and clear and shining, and also gold.

"Of the metals, Mars has red copper and all kinds of sulfur and has part of glass and premonada, and bloodstone and part of carnelian and onyx and in all stones that are red and tawny or speckled.

"Of the metals, the Sun has Egyptian glass and azernec and the stones albezedi and diamond and red pearls and stones that are sparkling and clear and part of hematite and azumbedich and ruby and the balassus ruby and gold marcasite.

"Of the metals, Venus has ruby and part of silver and glass and blue stones and coral and malachite and has part of quartz and lodestone.

"Of the metals, Mercury has quicksilver and part of tin and glass, and of stones it has emerald and all stones of this type and has part of azumbedich.

"The Moon of the metals has silver and silver marcasite and seed pearls and has part of crystal and blue stones and onyx and quartz."

—*Picatrix* II:10

Commentary below.

Picatrix likes to scatter knowledge across multiple lists and chapters to cause mischief among readers who do not read the book thoroughly. You will find electional rules, for example, strewn randomly in the later passages of the book where you least expect them. So it's not just a compilation artifact.

The Venus listing is fairly straightforward with the exception of blue stones. This is actually not any blue stone but both lapis lazuli and sapphire. Lapis lazuli simply means blue stone in Latin and sapphire means blue stone in Sanskrit, and over the years their traits became somewhat fused in spite of being very different minerals. The distinction is that lapis lazuli is good for melancholy and sapphire is good for protection against many, many things.

One of *Picatrix's* seemingly radical positions is to associate iron with Saturn. This is actually pretty logical, because Saturn governs hardness and heaviness, and iron is heavy like lead but far harder than it. It also oxidizes black. The association between lead and Saturn is from alchemy, and is a bit sloppy **IMHO**.

In Mercury I also don't know what "azumbedich" might be. It's impossible to engrave on quicksilver obviously, so the implementation of that is not possible. I *am* surprised by the inclusion of tin here. And the listing of emerald here is interesting because it provides a rationale for the substitution of green jasper and other green stones for emerald, in the context of Mercury.

The Moon lists silver, which is obvious, seed pearls which I'm not sure what those are, blue stones which as before are lapis lazuli and possibly sapphire- since these stones look like the colors of lakes and oceans and the Moon is the most watery of the planets. Quartz crystal looks like clear water. Quartz is definitely a Lunar Mansion option, and "blue stones" explains why lapis lazuli is used for a Lunar talisman later in the book.

And lastly, onyx is an interesting choice, but as the Moon is not a Benefic there are uses for a malevolent stone like this one in a Lunar context. Just don't make an onyx Lunar talisman expecting it will be friendly and helpful. Onyx here is surprising until you read what the lapidaries say it does. The traits of Al Gorab in the QS are effectively the same as onyx, and that's Martial in character in spite of the black color. Onyx is a fairly obvious association, especially if we bear in mind that in this context it's black or black banded onyx and not the other variations.

Onyx was a bit of a surprise, but the Moon is closely associated with mirrors and black polished surfaces do make good mirrors and were used as such in ancient times. If you make a Lunar onyx talisman, make sure it's the real stone. Most real onyx is black with white striations, not pure black. Most stones sold as onyx are actually commoner stones boiled in ink.

Red copper going to Mars makes some sense, because it's red and not everything Martial is a weapon.

When *Picatrix* mentions sulfur in an unusual context, remember that chemistry and metallurgy were primitive then and this could actually be a yellow-red stone of some other sort. I don't know what premonada is nor if it will be identified. Cameo is very likely chalcedony, which cameos are often made from. It's one of my preferred Saturn materials these days. Yellow marcasite is modern golden iron pyrite. What is called marcasite today is not medieval marcasite.

There's nothing surprising on the list for Jupiter except his association with lead. I can only think it's there because lead sheets were used for writing, and Jupiter governs part of the intellect and philosophy. Silver marcasite is silvery iron pyrite, which is one of my go-to gemstones these days due to its durability and availability. I also don't know what red pearls may be, but I speculate that they could be red coral.

I would have guessed that hematite is actually bloodstone, but bloodstone is already listed so it probably isn't. Hematite is a very brittle stone and is bad for jewelry. Gold marcasite here is of course golden iron pyrite. Balassus ruby is a type of spinel. Azernec is identified as a copper oxide. You'd think green copper would be Venereal, but it's Solar here.

I am coming of the opinion that lodestone is co-ruled by the Sun. It commands iron to move from a distance.

Picatrix page 66: "They say that the Moon has qualities from which it is possible to know and understand all her qualities and effects. The first of her qualities is her elongation from the Sun, that is, the period from the time she separates from conjunction with the Sun until her first square with the Sun. During that time her power increases moisture and warmth, but she affects moisture more than warmth. During that time her effects appear in the growth of trees and plants, and her power of increase is more apparent in herbs that grow in the ground than in trees that rise above the ground."

This section is partially in a code of a sort. It requires a certain amount of decryption for a modern reader. Note that it says *all* her qualities and effects. It's not just about agriculture, minerals and livestock, that's a way of misleading the casual reader.

Firstly, when *Picatrix* uses the term "heat," that's probably best translated as energy or speed. "Moist" means malleability and flexibility. After all, the element of fire is not the same thing as terrestrial fire, nor elemental water the same thing as terrestrial water. They indicate key characteristics which suffuse in the Sublunar world which have some resemblances to heat, cold, dryness and moisture. It is dangerous to believe this is literal, and very helpful to observe when it is otherwise.

When *Picatrix* says that the Moon in the first phase benefits herbs on the ground over trees that rise, what it is actually saying is that this phase is more conducive to variability and malleability than it is to strength and extent. To clarify, it means that the first phase of the Moon is more conducive to changing things and making things than it is to improving the strength and power of things which already exist in their proper form. To give an example, the first phase would be good for love and wealth, but better for love. Why? Because it is the generation of something new, rather than the increase of something already present.

Things can be associated with a star or planet because of similarity or a tempering quality. Furthermore, it may have associations based on some additional rationale.

Jupiter is warm and moist, but if all of his stones were equally so they would all behave the same. Furthermore, emerald falls under Jupiter, Mercury, and Spica; associations of all things among planets, elements, and stars are independent. Much as the feet are of the Moon but also Pisces, and the head of Mercury and Aries.

In this case, focusing on Signs and sears may lead us astray. We need the particular qualities of stones based on their purported proprieties, over other layers of association and sympathy.

Planetary Fragrances

When *Picatrix* refers to incense without qualification, especially with the implication that this is a solid or semi-solid substance, it is almost certainly jet (petrified wood) or amber. Jet and amber were used as incenses, and emit a gentle scent at room temperature, but they were also engraved as amulets in many cultures over many centuries.

In one instance *Picatrix* says to embed something in softened incense- this can't be jet, because it's impossible to soften that but you can soften resins such as amber. If you have to pick between the two, it's probably amber. It's in the same resin incense space as gum mastic, frankincense, and the almost-odorless gum arabic (acacia gum.)

While *Picatrix* does mention amber separately in many lists, its popularity justifies its basis as a genericized incense resin and amulet.

In addition to amber and jet being used both ways, sulfur was also placed in hollowed objects as amulets of protection. Sulfur was burned for exorcisms, and the powder or crystal would have been understood to retain the natural virtue – even though the crystals would be far too brittle to engrave upon. Sulfur is toxic when burned and is a scent offensive to humans as well as spirits it seems, and jet does not have a good scent either though it is mild. Amber is pleasant but very subtle.

There are only the most circumstantial and speculative historical connections between Scholastic Image Magic and African-American Conjure, or Hoodoo, yet I have seldom seen two very different traditions create such amazing synergy when properly combined.

The most frequent implementations of this synergy I have used are the feeding of **SIM** talismans with Hoodoo condition oils in a manner similar to feeding mojo bags, the magnification of the power of Hoodoo oils, powders, baths and natural curios by placing them temporarily in the proximity of compatible **SIM** talismans, and the creation of Hoodoo formulae and mojos which incorporate astrological talismans. To me, these are fairly straightforward combinations which make a lot of sense in the context of Al Kindi's theory of stellar and terrestrial rays, and the odd fusions of celestial and natural magics which appear in the writings of Cornelius Agrippa.

But going beyond relatively fundamental research into further optimization of these hybrids is what I have begun to explore. These explorations include the usage of magical fragrances on the body as supplementation for suffumigations used in astral petitions which appear in *Picatrix*, and the selection of fragrances to extend and maximize the potency of **SIM** talismans one may wear or carry.

Picatrix advises preparing for a planetary petition or talisman by consuming foods associated with that planetary hierarchy for as long as is manageable prior to the ritual. One manner of doing this in the case of Venus is by eating the animals of that planet such as goat, rabbit, deer or veal calf. Another is by using sweet and savory sauces. By consuming things that resonate with a particular planetary hierarchy, one harmonizes with it and, in a sense, one's body gradually becomes similarly composed.

This process can be enhanced by using fragrances compatible with the planetary hierarchy in question, either by association through the incenses used in the suffumigation of the planet, like frankincense essential oil in place of frankincense grains for Solar rites, or the sensory similarity between the scent and the associated flavors, thus an intensely sweet and grass-spicy blend of scents for Venus.

For example, as William Lilly says of Venus: "In Savours she delightes in that which is pleasant and toothsome; usually in moyst and sweet, or what is very delectable; in smels what is unctious and Aromatical, and incites to wantonnesse."

Scent is associated with the Air Element and will help the magician both receive and project planetary power of the associated type. Suffumigations, and thus scents of all kinds, are a foundational pillar of **SIM**. The complexity and potential for their ritual usage is almost inexhaustible, as the many recipes for such in *Picatrix* reveal.

This can be complicated by the fact that Hoodoo formulae have specific associations with olfactory signatures as well as sets of herbs and curios in the bottles. Hoodoo condition oil formulas have their own grammar and poetry, combining the meaning of scents and curios to produce unique variations of effect. It is my belief that the roots and curios produce terrestrial rays which are projected into the fragrances and impregnate them with signatures. When utilized, the Air element carries the scent and the signature of the curios into the wider universe to cause change.

When combining planetary work with Hoodoo, one can find some marvelous Hoodoo formulae which are entirely compatible with planetary work. For example, Commanding Oil and many of its cousins have strong Solar associations by scent, by function, by label imagery, and by curio. Placing a bottle of this near Solar talismans and then anointing yourself with it will not only give you a regal bearing that will accrue respect, but also make spirits of the Solar hierarchy find affinity with you and enhance the power of any Solar talismans you may be wearing.

Coherence, however, is power. It is not an uncommon practice to use more than one Hoodoo fragrance at once. I use at least three daily: for protection, for prosperity, and for love or authority. Some Hoodoo products can be used for numerous purposes, like Van Van Oil and Fast Luck. This can create problems with regard to planetary work.

When working in SIM styles of planetary magic, one needs to utilize objects or contexts where the particular planet or star's rays can fully permeate and ensoul an object, person, situation or even idea. Much like X-rays pass through flesh with ease, bone more difficultly, and metallic lead hardly at all, everything has a different capacity to receive or absorb animating power from one or more stellar hierarchies. Gold receives the rays of the Sun and Saturn very well, and Mars poorly. A soldier receives the rays of Mars well, the Sun moderately, and the Moon and Jupiter poorly. An idea for a novel receives the rays of Mercury and the Moon well, and Mars and Saturn poorly.

This concept of "reception" permeates *Picatrix's* theoretical discourses and causes confusion because the same term in English is used to describe certain planetary configurations. Reception is often understood to be (at least partially) a function of elemental qualities; so that things which fall under the power of the Sun have some affinity with those of Mars because both are hot and dry, and less so with the Moon which is cold and wet. Reception is a concept which replaces correspondence, so that every material or situation can become a vehicle for (or storage for) spiritual power, but to extremely variable degrees based on what flavor of celestial power is being utilized. It's hardly ever a 1:1 association; that notion was borrowed somewhat sloppily from alchemy, which functions quite differently.

Another bottleneck on reception is whether any particular thing is a combination of two or more components together, and whether each fall under the same or differing celestial hierarchies. The more pure a specific planet's associations are in any particular context, the stronger its hold over things in our world.

When planetary forces are mixed up too much, the power becomes muted and suppressed. It is the exact opposite of the notion of hybrid vigor. It is why magicians have done rituals to planets using consistent associations. The reason we don't dress in blood red for Mars, use a Venereal incense, wear a brass crown of the mind for Mercury and black snakeskin boots for Saturn during a ritual to Jupiter and thereby gain the benefits of five planets rather than one is that this doesn't work at all. It's like riding a chariot with the horses running in completely different directions; you go nowhere fast.

When planetary forces are coherent and particularly pure, they have a greater ability to express themselves, much like a planet on the cusp of an Angular Mundane House. This is of course independent of Essential Dignity, so having Saturn in Leo expressing itself with maximal freedom is usually a terrible idea. One of the essential goals of celestial magic in Scholastic Image Magic is to maximize this purity, or coherency. The effects become concentrated like a laser beam, and vastly more powerful.

This has relevance to the use of fragrances with planetary associations. If you use multiple fragrances, they should all have close associations with the planetary hierarchy you are working with. When you use scents that fall under two or more hierarchies, you will gain the benefits of each, but they will all produce muted results. If you instead use several magical scents that fall under a single planetary hierarchy, each will have greater power. Furthermore, any magics you perform when you have been using scents connected to a consistent singular hierarchy for days will be greatly enhanced.

Scholastic Image Magic is a tradition which cannot exist in modernity without modification. While we practitioners aspire to be maximally Traditional, we all have necessary adaptions and minor heresies. Not many people are following *Picatrix's* instructions on how to create an oracular head by waylaying a traveler and pickling their corpse, alchemical oil of feces sounds highly unpalatable, bullock sacrifices are expensive and challenging in an urban environment, and preserved antelope marrow is impossible to find, even on eBay. (I know. I've tried.)

Hoodoo has two qualities that make it useful to act as a plaster in the missing spaces where we cannot replicate what medieval and Renaissance men had access to. It is generally quite inexpensive; its most exotic ingredients are even less challenging than obtaining high quality lignum aloes. It is also a very successful adaption of traditional sorceries to the flora and fauna of North America, with reasonably well developed understandings of the signatures and properties of local resources.

But beyond this, magics of various traditions must to some extent exist in the same reality. Perhaps some operate on different planes of existence or operate on different principles rather than simply quirks of history, but there cannot be an infinitude of variants of magic which all function completely independently. Some must be capable of interacting, and interacting in a helpful manner.

I believe Scholastic Image Magic and Hoodoo are among the most compatible in their interactions; an elegant collaboration of High Magic and Low Magic which wildly transcends the definitions and limitations of each.

Optimizing Your Talismans

The primary tool for making SIM talismans is the diamond-tipped stylus or pen (I mean, other than your brains, astrology software and so forth.) Steel tips are not ideal if there's any chance you're going to work with harder minerals. Save yourself frustration and just go with the diamond tipped ones. If you make a lot of talismans, you can expect to replace your stylus two or three times a year, so to save on shipping order at least two. The harder the material engraved, the sooner the diamond tip dulls.

Do not use a dremel or another powered engraving tool. It will slide across the surface of the metal or gemstone, ruining the inscription or snagging it and slinging it across the room like a bullet. You do not want to find out what that's like.

Always test the condition of your stylus before the election, or have a backup ready. Good elections are too precious to fuck up.

Quick and dirty trick: If you need to have an image in red wax, buy a large red novena candle and remove as much of the wax as you can with a fork. Put the lumps and granules of wax into silicone cupcake cups that are removable from their metal tray. Take the silicone cups and put them in a microwave oven for about ten minutes or until the wax is thoroughly melted. Then, let it cool down for a few minutes, run your hands under cold water, and then transfer the silicone cups into a nearby freezer- putting them on the flattest possible surface. Within a half hour you should be able to pop the red wax disks out of the silicone and engrave on front and back during your election. Presumably this works just as well with black or white wax, of course. One advantage of this is that the disk is really closer to a cupcake so the thickness will make the talisman less prone to breakage.

The reason why silk cloth is used so frequently in magic is not primarily that it is a sign of respect to spiritual powers by dint of its expense and pleasantness-it is because it comes from a manner of animal which undergoes metamorphosis, and the power of metamorphosis is lent to the magic through contact with it.

Picatrix says that if the Pars Fortuna is cadent, it is bad for every kind of business.

Page 72, *Picatrix*. "Be sure in all judgments and elections that the Part of Fortune is not cadent from an aspect or conjunction with the Moon, and be careful that neither the lord of the Part of

Fortune's house nor the part itself is cadent from the ascendant after making an aspect with the ascendant or Moon. Now if the lord of the ascendant is conjunct the part of fortune, this is very good in all workings and all your elections. Take diligent care in all your workings that the Moon be not in the third, sixth, eighth, or twelfth houses from the Part of Fortune, because this will be ill and inappropriate for every manner of business."

Some of this is simplified by putting the Moon on the MC, because the Moon then is angular and it's easier to figure out what's cadent.

The Mansion position of the Moon also alters the flavor of any election, even in non-Mansion elections. If you're making a love talisman with Venus, and the Moon is in the 9th Mansion, it's going to be a little bit rougher. The PoF cannot be cadent from the Moon, but only in the adjacent House-if I'm reading the text correctly. Which means if I'm putting the Moon on the MC, it simply cannot be in the 9th House. If I'm right, that frees up a lot of elections I might have otherwise ruled out- two out of three, theoretically. The logic of this is more reasonable to me; it's similar to the idea that the Moon should not be separating from an aspect to a planet in whose domicile she is within.

I also don't ever give out elections or identify elections that I hope to use, in advance. The awareness of non-participants seems to suppress the efficacy of the talisman. Secrecy has properties in magic which are very unusual and cannot be dismissed out of hand, beyond the practical value.

Picatrix, page 49: "Next, it necessarily is required that the working of these operations be hidden from other people and from the light of the Sun, nor should they be done in any place where the Sun may enter, and no other person should learn about your workings, unless it be one who is faithful to you and believes in the work, neither a mocker nor a disbeliever in the work and the powers of the spirits of heaven, or in their powers having power in this world, or that the work is done by these spirits."

I just use drapes, blinds, or in extremis a pack of Post It Notes to block off direct sunlight. I don't find that dim, indirect sunlight causes problems.

Regarding the Moon, observe *Picatrix* page 67: "...the Moon reveals the Sun's influence and brings forth works accomplished by the Sun; nor do these appear until the Moon manifests those things that were previously concealed, and illuminates what had previously been in obscurity."

As I see it, a major purpose of the Sun is to command things and order things; therefore, a significant role of the Moon- maybe its most important one- is to control things. After all, elsewhere *Picatrix* says that the state of the Ascendant governs the beginning of things and the state of the Moon governs their ultimate conclusion.

While Scholastic Image Magic talismans do depend on specific timing for elections, there are some solutions if there is no proper election accessible for certain situations.

Page 148-149: "Then you should take some of the metal attributed to the planet, and from it cast a cross, doing this when the heavens are appropriately arranged; and set up the cross on two feet. Then combine it with a figure or image appropriate to your intention and the planetary spirit. For example, if you wish to make an image for battles or to conquer and terrify enemies, join the cross to the image of a lion or a snake...

"The reason why we have said that this figure should be made in the form of a cross is for reasons already given, that is, that the powers of all things are collected in figures that accord with the qualities that are in them, and flee from their contraries. We seek the powers of a planetary spirit in order that it may be united with a figure, but we do not know the form of the spirit, nor are we able to attain to that knowledge experimentally except in the form of a human being, an animal, or some other thing.

"It may be concluded from this that all the aforementioned virtue manifests most completely in figures. Therefore, we see all the figures and forms of trees and plants to be diverse in their shapes, just as the forms of animals are, and likewise minerals. As we have no way to perceive the proper forms of the planetary spirits, the ancient masters of this art chose the cross as a universal figure for them. This is because every body is perceived by its surfaces, and the surfaces of forms have length and breadth, and the proper figure of length and breadth is found in the cross. Thus we say that this shape has a universal magistery in these workings, and is as it were a receptacle for the powers of the planetary spirits insofar as the other figure does not diverge from them. This is one of the secrets of this art."

If this is in any way unclear, this implies that if one is creating a talisman and the image is not specified in any text, one is to engrave a depiction of one's goal at the center of an X with the lines exactly perpendicular and of equal length, as the X will be adequate to attract the stellar sympathy desired and embed the spirit being into the talisman. It's a heck of a shortcut, and a way of creating *many* new talismans with highly specific objectives. A big deal.

This is a good example of how one can repair a seemingly vile talismanic election and make it viable.

I made seven of these this morning; two rings for clients, a pendant and four rings for me. All were snow quartz in gold. The suffumigation was rose petals and the herb beneath was valerian. The engraving was one of the Venus images in *Picatrix*. Planetary dieting was initiated yesterday and continued through the night.

The Moon was very fast, but copresent with the South Node albeit far away. MSR was angular. The Moon was making a very tight sextile with Jupiter. Venus was Ascending in her middle degrees, and it was in her day and hour.

But oh no! The Moon is making an opposition with Mars. It's likely within orb too. This election is ruined!

Yet it is not.

The aspect perfects in the next Sign, so this diminishes its power. Furthermore Mars is cadent; in fact he's on the 3rd House cusp. *Picatrix* says that to rectify the Moon, put its affliction in a cadent house and a Benefic on the Ascendant. And look there, Venus is already on the Ascendant as this is a Venus talismanic election.

This is why it's a lot easier to elect for talismans of the Benefics than the Malefics.

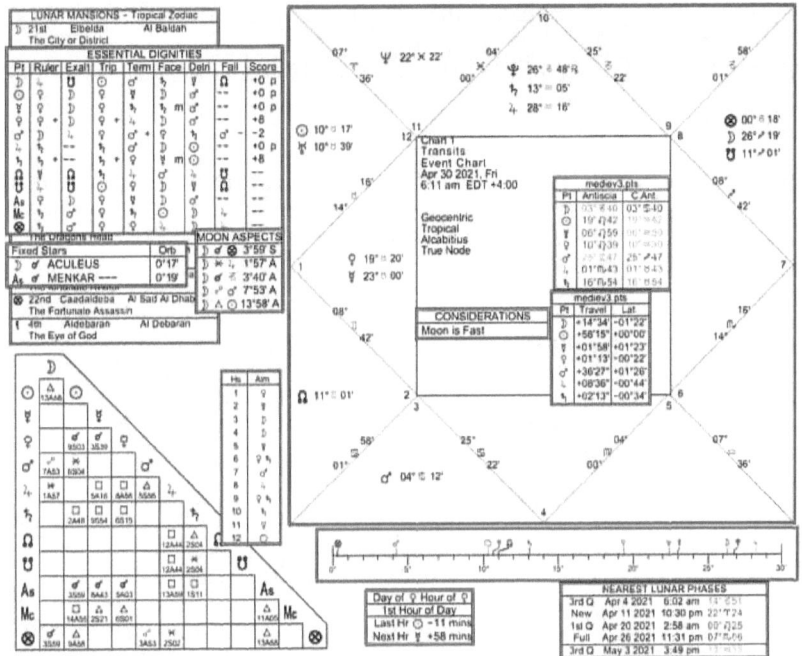

Planetary Antipathies and Substitutions

The *Picatrix*, *De Radiis Stellarum*, and *Three Books of Occult Philosophy* are the closest to broad textbooks of this tradition of Astrological Magic, but they are not meant to be used entirely by themselves. Both canonical texts of Astrological Magic and their partners, the manuals of traditional astrology, repeatedly state that the student must go beyond a mere rote understanding of formulae and considerations. The following step is the internalization of celestial functions, then a series of flashes of insight revealing why things are arranged as they are, and finally the integration of the practitioner into their proper spiritual hierarchy by the attainment of Perfect Nature and the maximization of their unique potential.

Authors are quite evasive about the aforementioned epiphanies for good reason; they allow teachers to recognize genuine insights arising from their better students that stand apart from the shallow mimicry that is the hallmark of pseudo-intellectualism, and they protect the secrets of the art from immature people who are at high risk of abusing it. Scholastic Image Magic has reputed power within it so vast that it can collapse entire civilizations if deployed with precision and ill intentions. Based on some of my experiences, I am certain that this is no idle boast. Some of the difficulty is deliberate in these texts, because of the gravity of that power falling into the wrong hands. It was the reasonable hope of the guardians and transmitters of this tradition that intellectual mastery developed roughly in tandem with emotional stability and personal responsibility.

Nevertheless, this has led to an incredibly steep learning curve for mastery of Scholastic Image Magic for modern students. Some of this is accidental and needs to be remedied, and some of this is very appropriate. As an example of the latter, it's critically important that a student be fully immersed in the traditional worldview, and at least provisionally set aside the modern worldview, so they may navigate deeply within this paradigm. This commentary is, I hope, an additional guide through one of the more important winding passages deeper into the heart of this complex system of magic and mysticism.

Let us begin with something highly counterintuitive and use it as a pretext to dive into some of the more practical and mystical secrets of the operations of celestial magic.

During a recent Solar talismanic election, I created two sets of talismans which were made at the same time. In addition to a set of bloodstones, I created two sapphire talismanic rings and a loose gemstone sapphire talisman. The herbs when applicable and suffumigations were identical. One of the rings is mine, and one ring and the loose gemstone will eventually be sold to clients or given to friends.

The inspiration for this talismanic project came from Eric Purdue's masterful new translation of Cornelius Agrippa's Book One of Three Books of Occult Philosophy. Agrippa frequently has long lists of gemstones, materials and animals which belong to the various celestial hierarchies, but less frequently highlights the particular powers attributed to each within that particular hierarchy's context. Agrippa gave very special attention to the gemstone he calls heliotrope that we believe is modern bloodstone, but also gave great attention to a gemstone called hyacinth in the J.F. translation. Eric Purdue, I believe correctly, provisionally identified hyacinth as modern sapphire. And with it come a list of powers which only apply in a Solar context; they are only activated when made into Solar talismans.

"Sapphires also have a solar virtue against poisons and pestilential vapors. When carried [the person] is rendered safe and acceptable, brings wealth and talent, and strengthens the heart. When held in the mouth, [sapphires] exceedingly cheer the mind."
-TBOC, Agrippa I:23, Eric Purdue trans.

Before I break down the rather long and fascinating list of powers attributed to Solar sapphire talismans, I must make mention of something of which most traditional (and Vedic) astrologers and readers of medieval lapidaries are quite aware. Sapphires have an extremely ancient and strong association with the planet Saturn, vastly more than the Sun. The association between sapphires and Saturn is so strong that due to what appears to be a confusion with lapis lazuli, the latter is associated with Saturn among other planets—sapphire appears to mean "blue stone" in Sanskrit, and lapis lazuli means the same in Latin. Though the Sun and Saturn do rule a few things in common, such as the metal gold and kingship, they are in most other ways complete opposites. There's nothing obviously Solar about sapphires; they are hard and usually dark stones—an obvious choice for the harsh, implacable, and dim Greater Malefic. Materials having multiple rulerships are not unusual, but this instance stands apart.

So is it a mistake? I'm quite sure it isn't. It's a phenomenal example of celestial antipathy which is described in *Picatrix* in more general terms about talismans which attract and repel animals.

"The effects upon animals are twofold—that is, one is to gather them and increase their number, and the other is to disperse and repel them. These are appropriate for different times, as they involve different motions—that is, there is a time for gathering and growth, and a time for dispersing and repelling. This may be considered under the heading of the opposition of degrees. In stones a certain supreme secret is hidden, that is, when any animal—that is, if you want it to depart—is hot in its nature, the stone ought to be cold; if the animal is moist, the stone ought to be dry, and vice versa. From this it should be understood that if you wish vipers and wasps to flee, the work ought to be done in cornelian and diamond and the like; but if they are cold by nature, such as scorpions, beetles, flies, lice, and things similar to them, work with hot stones such as malachite and crystal, and in bronze and gold and the like.

"This is for the working to make them flee. Workings to draw and increase them ought to be done with things that are harmonious and pertinent to them, as in working with vipers, you should work with gold and bronze and similar things. All this happens because of the harmony of complexion, the direction of movement, and the diversity of conjunctions and substances. The figure and form ought to be in the form and figure of the animal for which it is made, as a figure for mice in the shape of a mouse, one for serpents in the shape of a serpent, or one for scorpions in the shape of a scorpion."
–*Picatrix* IV:4, Greer-Warnock trans.

When *Picatrix* uses phrases like "a supreme secret" it's not just talking about talismans that act as mosquito repellant. It's an attempt to draw the discerning reader to a very important general principle that can be applied to a much wider set of circumstances. *Picatrix* uses language like this in other sections, such as the chapter on the manufacture of the thirty-six talismans of the Faces, to hint at a fairly radical reinvention of Neoplatonic cosmology that I have lectured upon previously. It is a test, an attempt to challenge the reader to learn a deeper lesson that is both mystical and extremely useful.

One of the concepts *Picatrix* describes elsewhere is what it sometimes calls reception: the capacity of a material to absorb celestial rays of a particular type. Some materials are receptive to the rays of many hierarchies. Emerald is receptive to Spica, Jupiter, Mercury and Moon. Silver is highly receptive to nearly every hierarchy because of the virtually ubiquitous and special role of the Moon in talismanic elections. Others are mostly inert, like clay, and to a lesser extent human flesh. (Clay talismans really do not work, and in spite of the obvious allure, talismanic tattoos aren't especially viable.)

Parallel to reception is "temperament" or temperateness: in modern expressions, the capacity for something to manifest normalcy, in contrast with manifestations which are abnormal and disruptive. Jupiter is the most temperate planet ,and usually signifies positive normalcy and health, and Mars is probably the least temperate planet, and usually signifies disruption and injury. Materials belonging to each of these hierarchies often share these attributes, but can increase or decrease them or channel them in a particular direction.

Related to the preceding are sympathy and antipathy: some materials attract and repel species based upon their inner natures. But what *Picatrix* is hinting at is that it isn't just animals that can be attracted by gemstones of one type and repelled by another, but also types of people, and finally even types of events. That's where it gets really interesting.

And that is how we return to sapphires.

Solar sapphire talismans have the following powers:

- They neutralize poisons.
- They protect against contagious diseases i.e. "pestilential vapors."
- They render the bearer safe from harm.
- They render the bearer inoffensive and pleasant.
- They attract riches.
- They magnify skills.
- They grant courage and health or "strengthen the heart."
- They act as antidepressants, especially if sucked upon.

Now you can tell why I prize these talismans at least as much as the bloodstone ones I created along with them. Fame, glory, constancy, invisibility, and restored youth are really great, but the eight powers listed above are possibly even more valuable for the average person.

What's even more interesting is what these powers tell us about sympathy and antipathy in celestial magic.

Generally speaking, the Sun is not the planet one would expect a cure for poisons from; that's more often associated with Jupiter. The Sun is nearly as temperate as Jupiter, and they both grant vigorous health and presumably a resistance to contagions. The Sun often can accomplish the works of Mars and vice versa, so the Sun can protect—especially from witchcraft and evil spirits. The Sun co-rules gold, which for most of history was currency, and thus can attract riches. The increase of skills may make sense because the Sun is fiery, and fire quickens as it illuminates. The Sun definitely can grant courage, and often is associated with the heart. Finally, the Sun can certainly act as an antidepressant; St. John's wort has been known to be ruled by the Sun since at least medieval times because of this property. However, in spite of a temperate planet endowing a quality of normalcy, the Sun is less associated with blending in than standing out; often in a highly aggressive manner. The Sun is the king, and the king likes to conquer.

I believe there's something else at work here:

- Saturn rules poisons
- Saturn rules contagious diseases.
- Saturn rules infirmity.
- Saturn rules ugliness and things which are essentially unpleasant.
- Saturn rules poverty and desperation, in spite of the co-rulership of gold.
- Saturn rules senility and stupefaction.
- Saturn rules fear and cowardice.
- Saturn rather famously rules melancholia.

I think what makes far more sense is that the function of a Solar sapphire talisman is to ward against many of the negative attributes of Saturn, because of the fundamental disagreement of natures between the hierarchies of the Sun and Saturn. The Sun is hot; Saturn is cold. The Sun governs all that is light and bright; Saturn rules all that is dark and shadowy.

It's a fantastic example of how one can use the materials of a dissimilar hierarchy to neutralize the negative effects of a planet or star. And it's one of the greater secrets of this system of magic.

The seven traditional planets often have peculiar relationships with each other, as illustrated in the 45 aphorisms that are said to be derived from the *Secretum Secretorum:*

"38. The Sun abhors those things that pertain to Saturn, and the things that pertain to the Sun are abhorrent to Saturn." -*Picatrix* IV:4

There's a long list of substitutions and antipathies in this chapter that are less pertinent, but must be memorized to attain mastery in this art. There are no shortcuts on this one.

This system of planetary pairings appears in the passages on planetary petitions as well.

"If you find yourself in contemplation and sorrow, or in melancholy or grave illness, in anything just named, or in any thing that has already been mentioned as belonging to Saturn, and you ask for something that belongs to his nature, you may seek it from him in the manner we describe below, and you may also help yourself in your petition by means of Jupiter. The essence of all these petitions is that you should not seek anything from any planet unless it belongs to his dominion...

"Seek from Mars what is consistent with his nature, such as petitions against soldiers, officials, fighters, and those who busy themselves with warlike acts; and on behalf of friends of kings, and those who destroy homes and citizens, and do evil to humanity, killers, executioners, those who work with fire or in places such as stables, litigators, shepherds, thieves, companions on the road, liars, traitors, and the like. Similar, ask him concerning infirmities of the body from the groin downwards, and also for phlebotomy, accumulation of gas, and the like. In these latter petitions you may also help yourself with Venus, for the nature of Venus dissolves what is closed up by Mars, and repairs what he damages...

"Seek from Venus all things that pertain to her, such as petitions of women, boys, and girls, daughters, and generally everything pertaining to the love of women and carnal copulation with them, art, vocal and instrumental music, telling jokes, and all those who give themselves over to worldly pleasures, those who engage in vices, male and female servants, brides and grooms, mothers, friends, sisters, and all those similar to them, and in these petitions you may also help yourself with Mars." *- Picatrix* III:7

It also should be observed at this point that Jupiter and Saturn are oppositional in nature but are (slightly counterintuitively) "friends" with each other. The same is true of the hierarchies of Mars and Venus. The cliché of opposites attracting is reflected in celestial symmetries or harmonies. I believe that this system of substitutions using planets of oppositional nature but mutual amity goes even further than what *Picatrix* states explicitly. It says that Jupiter can substitute for Saturn, but not the reverse; it may be a somewhat reasonable assumption, however. To learn more about planetary substitution, we must look elsewhere.

For that, we turn our attention to the other Luminary: the Moon. In *Picatrix* II:10 there's a wonderful miscellany of planetary talismanic recipes, one of which I've made but never quite understood until fairly recently.

"If, under the influence of the Sun, you write the figures below in a sedina stone with the Sun rising in the first face of Leo, whoever carries this stone will be protected against the lunar illnesses that come from the combustion of the Moon."

Combustion (a close conjunction of a planet with the Sun) is deemed to be the worst planetary affliction according to William Lilly and is generally accepted as such in traditional astrology, with some uncommon exceptions. The combustion of the Moon is especially dire; it often signifies death and destruction in elections, and a variety of challenging health concerns in natal charts.

The more conventional suggestion would be to use a talisman of an afflicted planet in a person's natal chart as a remedy, but here we see something very different. Here the suggestion is to double-down on the influence of the Sun. It seems counterintuitive because the Sun is overwhelming the native's Moon, but it is logical if the Sun and the Moon have a similar relationship as Jupiter and Saturn have, and Mars and Venus mutually share in the petitional instructions cited above.

Indications that this is the case between the Sun and Moon are scattered throughout *Picatrix*.

"The Nabatean sages have said that the power and works of the heavens and stars are from the Sun originally, and this is because they see and understand that the Moon helps him (that is, as much as is in her power), while the Sun does not need her effects, nor those of the other planets; and similarly, the five other planets follow the Sun in their effects and obey and are humbled by him, and proceed in their aforementioned effects according to the dispositions of the Sun. In the same way, according to their opinion, all their effects are primarily rooted in the Sun, and the other six planets help him by their effects. Similarly, the fixed stars are the Sun's handmaidens, and serve, obey, and are humbled by him, and while they help him with their effects, this is not because of any need that he has of them." - *Picatrix* III:8

And elsewhere: "Our sages say likewise that the virtue of the fifth quality [the Moon in a perfected conjunction with the Sun] has a similar effect to the effect of the Sun, and this is a very great thing and a noble quality. They say that all composite bodies receive from this the virtues that they ought to have, nor should it be understood from the foregoing that the Moon causes virtues and workings differing from those of the Sun; rather, the Moon reveals the Sun's influence and brings forth works accomplished by the Sun; nor do these appear until the Moon manifests those things that were previously concealed, and illuminates what had previously been in obscurity." - *Picatrix* II:3

One of the ways *Picatrix* conceals secrets of talismanic magic is by describing electional considerations and the composition of talismans and suffumigations in what superficially appear to be abstract cosmological relationships. To a person immersed in the worldview espoused by the author, ultimately there is no difference between these things; or at least there is a profound sympathy.

While most talismanic and petitional elections depend strongly upon the condition of the Moon and to some extent the planet on or ruling the Ascendant, if a major significator in the election is the Sun, the role of every other planet is greatly diminished. The manifestation might be subtler with a weak Moon, however. In theory, one could create a benevolent Solar talisman even if the Moon was afflicted catastrophically. I personally wouldn't take that chance unless it were an emergency.

Tropical astrology is not heliocentric; it is geocentric. But it is also what I call heliophilic. It gives a very special significance to the role of the Sun, and it has powers unique among all the planets. It is not merely the strongest planet—something seldom stated in canonical texts because it really is taken for granted—but it has a central role in the cosmos as the bringer of order, the primary source of visible and astral light, the liminal mediator between the world of Forms and the Sublunar sphere, and of the four seasons that sustain all life. Thus, through the Sun, the equinoxes and solstices define the positions and properties of the Zodiacal Signs and the essential architecture of the universe and time itself.

Traditional celestial magic conceals a lot of secrets of both a practical and spiritual nature, and as we solve the puzzles it sets before us in the canonical sources, the aspiration is that our own personal disjointedness is transformed into a more coherent spiritual being. I'm cheating a little by letting you in on some of the glimpses of the treasures that I've uncovered. I'm hoping that you'll forgive me for bending the rules a little; that you'll return the favor someday to myself and others, and that you'll use this knowledge wisely.

No one can perfect any of the works of traditional Astrological Magic without passing on some of the illumination that one receives, much like the Sun illuminates each of the planets and they transmit their light and fill all of their hierarchies with vitality and power. It's more than a metaphor; it's the essential connection between consciousness and cosmos that produces magic and our experience of reality itself.

www.ingramcontent.com/pod-product-compliance
Lightning Source LLC
Chambersburg PA
CBHW032128160426
43197CB00008B/555